LORDS OF THE SITH

THE BEST OF *STAR WARS INSIDER*
GUIDE TO THE DARK SIDE

WWW.TITAN-COMICS.COM

Star Wars Insider
Lords of the Sith
ISBN: 978-1-78585-1919

Published by Titan
A division of
Titan Publishing Group Ltd.,
144 Southwark Street,
London, SE1 0UP

Collecting material
previously published in
Star Wars Insider magazine.

A CIP catalogue record for this title is available from the British Library.

First Edition April 2017
10 9 8 7 6 5 4 3 2 1

Printed in China.

Editor Jonathan Wilkins
Senior Executive Editor Divinia Fleary
Copy Editor Simon Hugo
Designer Russell Seal
Art Director Oz Browne
Senior Designer Andrew Leung
Publishing Manager Darryl Tothill
Publishing Director Chris Teather
Operations Director Leigh Baulch
Executive Director Vivian Cheung
Publisher Nick Landau

Acknowledgments
Titan would like to thank the cast and crews of the *Star Wars*
films, and the animated series: *Star Wars: The Clone Wars* and
Star Wars Rebels. A special thanks also to the teams at Dark Horse
Comics, Marvel Comics, and Del Rey for their contributions
to this book. A huge thanks also to Frank Parisi, Brett Rector, and
Michael Siglain at Lucasfilm for all of their help in putting this
volume together.

LORDS OF THE SITH

THE BEST OF *STAR WARS INSIDER*
GUIDE TO THE DARK SIDE

CONTENTS

EXCLUSIVE LIMITED EDITION COLLECTOR'S COVER

STAR WARS INSIDER#113
Dec 2009
US $7.99 CAN $9.99

INTRODUCTION OF A SITH LORD
DARTH VADER ARRIVES

ISSUE 113
DECEMBER 2009

The sight of a shadowy figure gradually growing larger until the terrifying visage of Darth Vader is revealed is one of many iconic character entrances in *A New Hope*. This powerful moment--in a film that delivers multiple powerful moments just minutes in--introduces audiences to their first Sith Lord. And, as this article reveals, it almost didn't happen!—**Jonathan Wilkins**

James Earl Jones *was born on January 17, 1931 in Arkabutla, Mississippi. He made his Broadway debut in 1957; and over the course of a career spanning more than 60 years, he has become one of the most well-respected and best-loved actors working today. Jones has won many accolades, including Tony and Golden Globe Awards for his role in* The Great White Hope *on Broadway (as well as being nominated for an Academy Award for Best actor in the film adaptation) and two Emmys for his roles in television productions:* Heat Wave *(1990) and* Summers End *(1999). He first voiced Darth Vader in 1977, and then later went on to win over a whole new legion of fans in 1994 when he voiced Mufasa in Disney's animated masterpiece,* The Lion King.

WORDS: BRIAN J. ROBB

WHY IT'S A CLASSIC....

The first entrance of Darth Vader in *Star Wars* needed to be spectacular. The script had to establish the menace of the main villain of the movie immediately, and in a few broad brush strokes. The all-black suit contrasted wonderfully with the already intimidating all-white armored stormtroopers, and the antiseptic white corridors of the Rebel Blockade Runner (a last minute addition, see: What They Said). Vader had instant presence and a cruel authority, which he wasn't hesitant to use against the Rebel crew and his own stormtroopers in order to achieve his aims. John Williams' musical fanfare accompanying his entrance helped immensely, too. Then the sounds of battle fell silent as the Dark Lord of the Sith surveyed the scene, the only sound being the eerie breathing noises coming from within that all-enclosing helmet. Then came the chilling voice and its expression of a single-minded aim: Find the Ambassador and find the plans, nothing else matters. Vader enjoyed a slew of classic moments throughout the *Star Wars* saga, but few of them were as important as this first entrance: It established everything we needed to know about the character in under a minute of screen time.

1977 Script

INT. REBEL BLOCKADE RUNNER—MAIN HALLWAY.
The awesome, seven-foot-tall Dark Lord of the Sith makes his way into the blinding light of the main passageway. This is Darth Vader, right hand of the Emperor. His face is obscured by his flowing black robe and grotesque breath mask, which stands out next to the fascist white armored suits of the Imperial stormtroopers. Everyone instinctively backs away from the imposing warrior and a deathly quiet sweeps through the Rebel troops. Several of the Rebel troops break and run in a frenzied panic.

INT. REBEL BLOCKADE RUNNER—CORRIDOR
The evil Darth Vader stands amid the broken and twisted bodies of his foes. He grabs a wounded Rebel Officer by the neck as an Imperial Officer rushes up to the Dark Lord.

WHAT THEY SAID

The white corridor into which the film's main villain Darth Vader makes his spectacular entrance was a late addition to the movie. Lucas directed production designer John Barry to construct the additional hallway in which he needed to stage the opening gun-battle.

"That created a whole big ruckus with Fox, because it cost a lot more money. Ultimately, as the director, if you decide it is vital to the film, it is vital to the film. We had to have it: I couldn't make the movie with half a set. I was very concerned that the opening, the first interior of the film, be spectacular and look opulent, and not just be a set redress. So John built a new white set."

George Lucas, *The Making of Star Wars: The Definitive Story Behind the Original Film*

ENTER DARTH VADER

CLASSIC MOMENT
STAR WARS: EPISODE IV
— A NEW HOPE
[DVD CHAPTER 03]

WHAT THEY SAID

"On the very first shot we did, I had to walk up a corridor. The camera was following me on track going all the way up the corridor. I had decided that Vader would have a brisk, purposeful stride, meaning that everybody had to trot quickly beside me to keep up. I strode to the end of the corridor and George Lucas said, "Sorry David, you've got to slow down. The camera can't keep up with you!""

David Prowse, Darth Vader,
Star Wars Insider #108

IMPERIAL OFFICER: The Death Star plans are not in the main computer.

Vader squeezes the neck of the Rebel officer, who struggles in vain.

VADER: Where are those transmissions you intercepted?

Vader lifts the Rebel off his feet by his throat.

VADER: What have you done with those plans?

REBEL OFFICER: We intercepted no transmissions. Aaah... This is a consular ship. We're on a diplomatic mission.

VADER: If this is a consular ship... where is the Ambassador?

The Rebel refuses to speak but eventually cries out as the Dark Lord begins to squeeze the officer's throat, creating a gruesome snapping and choking, until the soldier goes limp.

Vader tosses the dead soldier against the wall and turns to his troops.

VADER: Commander, tear this ship apart until you've found those plans and bring me the Ambassador. I want her alive!

The stormtroopers scurry into the sub-hallways. ☮

STAR WARS INSIDER
#113 Dec 2009
US $7.99 CAN $9.99

VILLAINS SPECIAL

ASKING ANAKIN | **EVIL DEEDS** | **THE OLD REPUBLIC**
MATT LANTER INTERVIEWED ! | *STAR WARS'* DARKEST MOMENTS | WE PREVIEW THE GAME THAT WILL BLOW YOUR MIND!

STAR WARS

**EXCLUSIVE
INTERVIEW!**
THE CLONE WARS
PRODUCER
CARY SILVER ON
SEASON TWO

JOIN US!
THE VILLAINS OF STAR WARS

KILL KENOBI!
HOW THE FORCE UNLEASHED:
ULTIMATE SITH EDITION
IS REWRITING HISTORY!

PALPATINE
DARTH SIDIOUS

ISSUE 113
DECEMBER 2009

THIS MONTH, FAR, FAR AWAY....

The Nightsister's Revenge, the 6th expansion of the *Star Wars* Galaxies Trading Card Game, released

Star Wars: The Thrawn Trilogy released

Family Guy: Something, Something, Something, Dark Side released on DVD

Darth Vader may be the most iconic screen villain of all time, but the most truly villainous of them all surely must be the polite senator from Naboo—a phantom menace indeed! Ian McDiarmid once remarked to me that, apart from his patronage of the arts (see *Revenge of the Sith*), there are no redeeming features to Palpatine (otherwise known as Darth Sidious, and then the Emperor). It's true: He's ruthless, conniving, powerful, and utterly set in his evil ways. There's no way this Sith Lord is going to redeem himself. He is, in short, pure evil.—**Jonathan Wilkins**

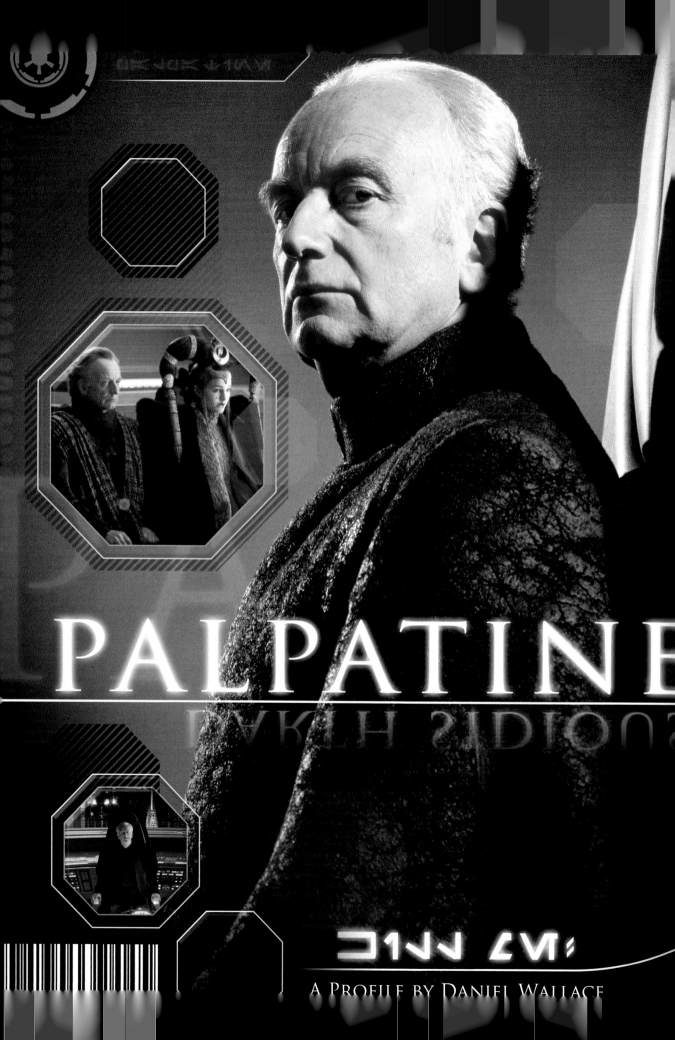

L ittle is known about the man who was inarguably the most important political figure of the galaxy's last thousand years. By design, all records of Palpatine's early life were purged from public records, and historians were forced to judge the man by the impact of his creations. No figure created more grandiose works than the self-proclaimed Galactic Emperor.

Palpatine is believed to have been born on Naboo, a quiet Mid Rim world in the Chommell sector. Apparently never trained by the Jedi despite his Force sensitivity, Palpatine instead fell under the influence of a Sith Lord, Darth Plagueis.

Under the Rule of Two—one Master, one apprentice—Plagueis sought to continue the tradition through Palpatine. After receiving the Sith title Darth Sidious, Palpatine studied the secrets of the dark side, including his Master's apparent ability to generate life by influencing midi-chlorians. Plagueis may even have succeeded, given the strange circumstances surrounding the birth of Anakin Skywalker. This did not matter to Palpatine, who had already taken his own apprentice in secret. Knowing there could never be more than two, Palpatine murdered Plagueis in his sleep, and concentrated on teaching the Zabrak boy he called Maul to become the perfect killer.

"THE SITH AND THE JEDI ARE SIMILAR IN ALMOST EVERY WAY. THE DIFFERENCE BETWEEN THE TWO IS THE SITH ARE NOT AFRAID OF THE DARK SIDE OF THE FORCE. THAT IS WHY THEY ARE MORE POWERFUL."

—PALPATINE, TO ANAKIN SKYWALKER

A DOUBLE LIFE

Palpatine maintained a double life, winning an election for Senator of the Chommell sector and relocating to Coruscant. His fellow politicians believed the new provincial could be safely ignored, but Palpatine possessed a gift for forging alliances and isolating his critics. His friends included Wilhuff Tarkin and Jedi Master Jorus C'baoth, while his aides Sate Pestage and Kinman Doriana covered up any evidence of impropriety.

Palpatine helped engineer the assassination of the Trade Federation directorate on Eriadu, and in his guise as Sidious he convinced the surviving Trade Federation leaders to blockade Naboo. The blockade and subsequent invasion brought Queen Amidala to Coruscant, where Palpatine convinced her to introduce a vote of no-confidence in Supreme Chancellor Valorum. When the crisis ended, Palpatine had lost Maul to Obi-Wan Kenobi's blade, but had gained something far more valuable—the chancellorship of the Republic. The Naboo incident also saw the public emergence of Anakin Skywalker, who Palpatine saw as a potential future apprentice.

Palpatine convinced the dissident Jedi Dooku to join his cause, giving him the title Darth Tyranus. While Dooku helped secure a clone army and spread the seeds of Separatism, Palpatine engineered the destruction of the Outbound Flight Project to kill the Jedi on board. The incident put him in contact with Thrawn, who would later be his greatest Grand Admiral.

After winning re-election twice, Palpatine convinced the public he should remain in office to oppose the Separatist movement of Count Dooku. With Palpatine and Dooku playing the roles of opposing commanders and plotting behind the scenes, the Senate gave the Supreme Chancellor emergency war powers. Palpatine used them to requisition the clone army that Dooku had set up, and the Clone Wars began.

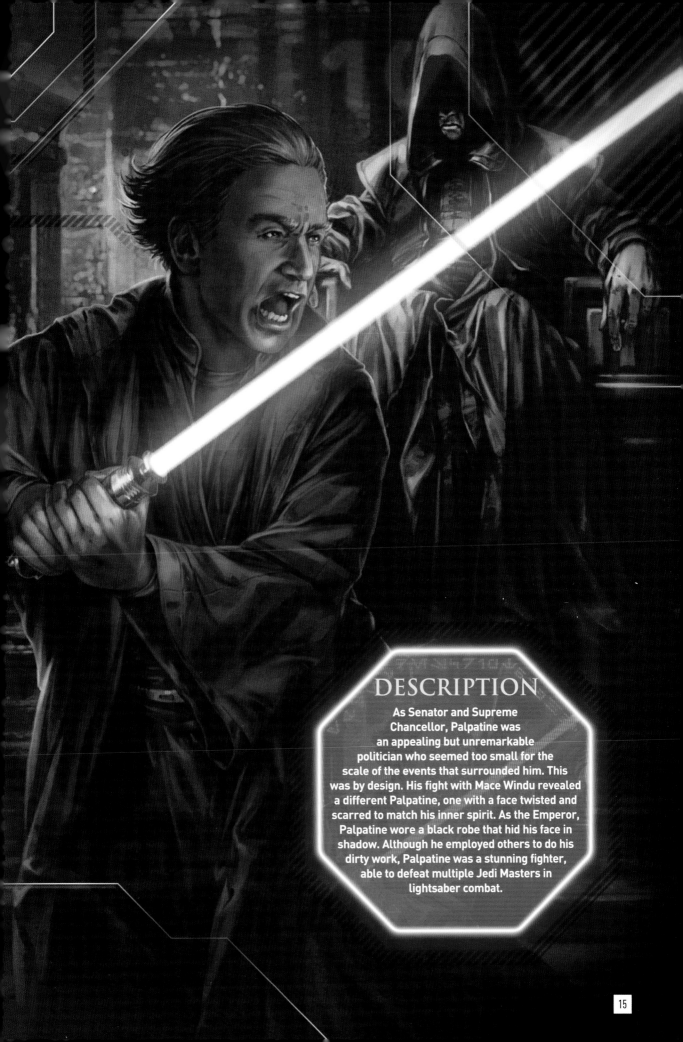

DESCRIPTION

As Senator and Supreme
Chancellor, Palpatine was
an appealing but unremarkable
politician who seemed too small for the
scale of the events that surrounded him. This
was by design. His fight with Mace Windu revealed
a different Palpatine, one with a face twisted and
scarred to match his inner spirit. As the Emperor,
Palpatine wore a black robe that hid his face in
shadow. Although he employed others to do his
dirty work, Palpatine was a stunning fighter,
able to defeat multiple Jedi Masters in
lightsaber combat.

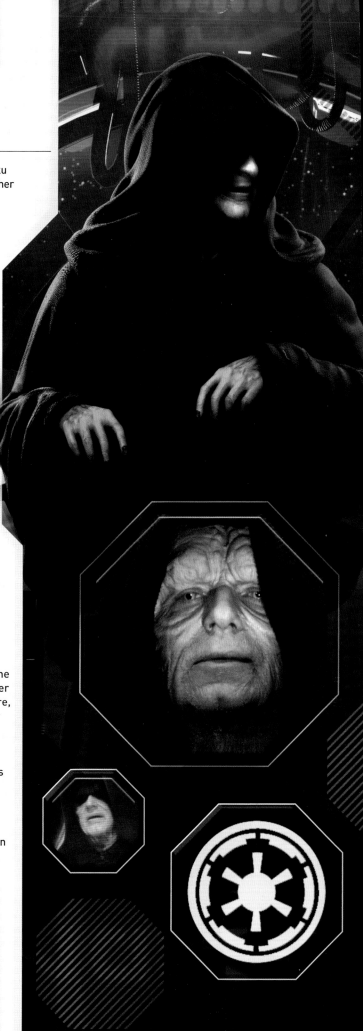

ENDGAME

Over the next three years Palpatine and Dooku kept the war carefully balanced so that neither side gained a clear advantage, but that the maximum number of Jedi perished in the crossfire. By the time of Palpatine's "kidnapping" at the hands of General Grievous, the war was at an end—and Palpatine didn't need Dooku anymore. In a lightsaber duel, Anakin Skywalker killed the Count and cleared the field for his own ascension into the ranks of the Sith. Skywalker proved his worth by assisting Palpatine in killing Mace Windu, and then led the raid on the Jedi Temple after receiving his new Sith name, Darth Vader. Not even Yoda could stop Palpatine's sinister plans, as the new Emperor exterminated most of the remaining Jedi by issuing Order 66 and announcing to the galaxy that the war's close marked the Empire's beginning.

Only one thing dimmed Palpatine's triumph. Darth Vader had lost a battle with Obi-Wan Kenobi at Mustafar, and required a cybernetic rebuild. His apprentice would now be more machine than man. Palpatine began considering replacements.

Meanwhile, the galaxy entered a golden age— for some. Renamed Imperial Center, Coruscant became the seat of Human High Culture, and Star Destroyers and TIE fighters maintained the security of the Core. Life was far less appealing for non-humans, who found themselves herded into segregated zones or conscripted to toil on the Death Star project. Some citizens protested, but Palpatine moved swiftly against any hint of rebellion. He would have executed the core of the Rebel leadership if not for the interference of Starkiller, Darth Vader's secret apprentice.

With the completion of the Death Star, Palpatine felt confident in dissolving the Imperial Senate. Though the battle station was destroyed during the Battle of Yavin, a bright spot in the defeat was the discovery of Vader's son Luke Skywalker. As the Rebel Alliance grew, Palpatine remained fixated on Skywalker as a replacement for Vader and ultimately lured the Rebels into a trap at Endor. There, aboard the second Death Star, he tried to turn Skywalker to the dark side of the Force. Skywalker's refusal so enraged Palpatine that he shot Sith lightning from his fingertips, painfully and slowly torturing him. But Vader hurled Palpatine to his death, using the last moments of his life to save his son.

In the following years Palpatine returned in a series of clone bodies, striking out at the New Republic using superweapons including the World Devastators and the Galaxy Gun, but ultimately succumbed to the deterioration of his clones and vanished into the Force forever. ☙

PALPATINE

STAR WARS INSIDER

An Interview with Prequel Star
Ian McDiarmid:
Senator Palpatine
Revealed

**Star Wars Actors
Peter Cushing and
Jack Purvis Remembered**

**Forget the Rumors
Real Prequel News on Page 10**

**Greedo Found Alive
and Living in California**

ISSUE 37 U.S.A. $4.50 CANADA $5.95

IAN McDIARMID
THE EMPEROR

ISSUE 37
APRIL/MAY 1998

THIS MONTH, FAR, FAR AWAY....

Crimson Empire 5 released

Young Jedi Knights: Return to Ord Mantell released

I, Jedi published

Tales of the Jedi: The Fall of the Sith Empire trade paperback released

Galaxy of Fear: The Doomsday Ship released

Crimson Empire 6 released

I've yet to be proved wrong on my theory that actors who are best known for playing villains are, in fact, some the nicest, gentlest people that you could hope to meet. It's a theory bolstered by Ian McDiarmid, who is far more likely to offer you tea than to demand power.

This vintage interview from 1999 takes us back to when McDiarmid reprised his role as Palpatine—last seen in *Return of the Jedi*—as a younger and seemingly nicer man in Episode I: *The Phantom Menace*. Veteran *Insider* contributor Scott Chernoff gets a fascinating interview from McDiarmid, who, over the years, has proved just as charming and forthcoming at a number of *Star Wars* Celebrations.—**Jonathan Wilkins**

Ian McDiarmid was born on August 11, 1944. A multi award-winning actor and director, he served as the artistic director at the Almeida Theatre in London and has appeared in numerous films including Sleepy Hollow *(1999) and* Dirty Rotten Scoundrels *(1989). His numerous TV roles include Professor Levi in* The Young Indiana Jones Chronicles *episode "Paris, October 1916."*

Ian McDiarmid.
interviewe

SOM
WIC
THS

He is a mystery, an untouchable enigma who commands the strongest currents of the Force in the service of the darkest visions of evil. In his quest for galactic domination, he turns star system against star system, father against son. He is Emperor Palpatine, the dark overlord who is destroyed by Darth Vader in Return of the Jedi. *And now, the Emperor is back.*

by Scott Chernoff
Illustration by Hugh Fleming

THING KED WAY COMES

Well, sort of. In Episode I of the new *Star Wars* trilogy, we rewind and go back in time to see then-Senator Palpatine begin his infamous rise to power. But unlike other familiar characters such as Obi-Wan Kenobi and Anakin Skywalker, Palpatine is once again played by the same brilliant actor who originated the role, Ian McDiarmid. (Clive Revill voiced a hologram of the character in *The Empire Strikes Back*.)

Bringing back McDiarmid—indeed, expanding his role—is a masterstroke for the prequel. In *Return of the Jedi,* McDiarmid, unrecognizable beneath layers of makeup, inhabited the character of the Emperor so completely that he made a powerhouse out of every offhand remark. (His coy take on "Oh… I'm afraid the deflector shield will be quite operational when your friends arrive" springs to mind.) »

*N*ot surprisingly, McDiarmid, who is now "just over 50," brought a wealth of experience to the role. A native of Scotland, where he grew up in the seaside town of Dundee, McDiarmid earned a masters degree in Social Science before shifting to the Royal Scottish Academy of Dramatic Arts, where he studied with fellow *Star Wars* icon Denis Lawson (Wedge), among others.

A successful London stage career soon followed, as did small roles in films such as *Dragonslayer* (1981) and *Gorky Park* (1983). Since making Jedi, McDiarmid has appeared in a handful of films, including 1995's Oscar-winning *Restoration* and 1988's Steve Martin/Michael Caine comedy *Dirty Rotten Scoundrels*, which was directed by Frank Oz (who plays McDiarmid's spiritual nemesis, Yoda, in the *Star Wars* saga).

But McDiarmid's attention has largely been focused on England's Almeida Theatre, where he has served as joint artistic director with Jonathan Kent, since 1990. When we talked to him, McDiarmid was on his way to a technical rehearsal for the theatre's new production and preparing to begin rehearsals for his lead role in the next.

Yet despite his hectic schedule, McDiarmid was kind enough to answer all of our questions about *Return of the Jedi* and Episode I—and there were a lot of questions. Luckily, many of the answers were still fresh in his mind, since principal photography on Episode I had wrapped only three weeks before…

*W*as it tough getting back into character 15 years later—and making him so much younger?

It's a rare experience, if not a unique one. Of course, in *Jedi*, the character was older. Now I have an opportunity to play myself younger than my own years, which has never happened to me before. So I suppose I'm getting to know this guy retrospectively.

How did you go about re-creating the character? Did you look back at your own performance in *Return of the Jedi*?

Like everybody else, I rushed to see the Special Edition, and I had a good time. But that was all I did, really. I remembered him. I remembered what he feels like quite clearly.

What does he feel like?

It's a part that's in some ways easy to play,

McDiarmid, *unrecognizable beneath layers of makeup, inhabited the character of the Emperor so completely that he made a powerhouse out of every offhand remark.*

because if you're playing someone who controls the universe, on the set you sit in a chair in the middle of the room, higher than everyone else. And [in *Jedi*] I was encased in quite a lot of makeup with yellow eyes, and in order to move and to eat and to facilitate everything, there was a whole number of people who would do that for me. So in a sense, the whole business of preparing for the part before going on camera got me into character.

As a classically-trained actor, how do you get inside that guy?

For me, it's really reading the script, talking to the people, and hoping that something will happen. And then you have to be in a state of readiness for it to happen. What's exciting is you're surrounded by so many people doing so many things, so the level of energy in the studio is always extremely high. These are literally the best people at what they do, so there's a prevailing level of excellence, and you just hope that some of that is going to rub off.

How much of a free reign were you given 15 years ago to create the character and come up with your own readings of the lines?

Well, all the readings of the lines were my

own. We'd discuss it—it was Richard Marquand who directed that, as you remember—and the way any director and actor would work together, we'd suggest things to each other.

How much back story did George Lucas give you on your character?

Very little, really. Like everybody else, I've read the books and worked things out, but I think it's quite good that I know as little as I do.

>> Ready to start filming on the set of Senator Palpatine's quarters on Coruscant are (left to right) Director George Lucas, Art Director Phil Harvey, 3rd Assistsant Director Ben Howarth, Camera Operator Trevor Coop, 1st Assistant Director Chris Newman and Director of Photography David Tattersall.

I'm left with the best tools really, which are just the lines, the other actors, and the situation. He's a mysterious, dark character, but that suits me and suits him, because I wouldn't want to do anything to dispel the mystery, or to lighten the darkness.

When you were filming *Jedi*, did you have any idea that you would be reprising your role 15 years later?

No. It was all a complete surprise to me in the first place, because I came into Jedi very late in the day. The then-casting director had seen me play much older than my years in a play by Sam Shepard called *Seduced*. I did that at the Royal Court Theatre Upstairs, which is a very small theatre, so we were very close to the audience.

McDiarmid, who played the frightening Emperor
...e in *Return of the Jedi*, returns to play his younger
...ator Palpatine, in *Star Wars*: Episode I.

>> Emperor Palpatine boards the Death Star from his shuttle. Just what was The Emperor wearing under those robes in *Return of the Jedi?* Actor Ian McDiarmid reveals "... Japanese black trousers and a T-shirt..."

for dark and black, you go deep. I knew it had to be deep, and a little animal-like—but a very sophisticated animal.

Which animal?

I don't know, it sort of moves around all the time. I thought he looked like a toad. That was toward the end of his life, and he was an extremely bitter and desiccated man. Earlier on, he was a flamboyant talent. I think the Emperor probably escaped bitterness. He didn't need to worry about being bitter, because there's nobody more powerful than him—except in the end of course, when suddenly his whole reliance on the doctrine of fear didn't pay off.

So the character came naturally to you?

This one, I don't know, it's easier than it should be. Because it's such a simple and direct story, it's somehow much easier than it often is to take it seriously. These are big, direct, almost naive emotions. For an actor these are always the ones that are the most exciting to play—and the most demanding. You know you've got to find them somewhere. There's no subterfuge to hide behind. You've just got to be direct if you're going to play the part properly.

Did you put a lot of thought into devolving him backward 36 years for Episode I?

No, not really. Early on, he's a successful politician, who seemingly wanted the best for his planet, and through that want, he might progress. So it was really a straightforward job. One just looks at contemporary politicians, and you do it as you'd play any straightforward, naturalistic part. But of course, I have in the back of my mind—and I dare say a large number viewing it as well in the back of theirs—the fact that in a number of years, this is the most evil person who's ever dominated a planet, let alone the universe.

He looks like a fun character to play. You had some very juicy lines in the last one.

Yes, very fun, and they're simple lines, which I like too. They're simple and straightforward and direct lines, and they don't really have any subtext. If you wield that kind of power, you don't need to bother with subtext. You say what you feel and enact what you feel.

Let's get this out of the way: what were you wearing under the robes?

[Laughs.] I think I was wearing a very dignified black outfit. I remember it quite well. It was sort of Japanese black trousers and a T-shirt.

Mary Selway [Buckley], who was the casting director, saw that and reckoned that I could play old convincingly in, as it were, close-up. That was why she recommended me to George and Richard, and they filled me in and had a very brief meeting, and before I knew where I was, I was playing the part.

Had you seen the other two *Star Wars* films before that?

I hadn't seen *The Empire Strikes Back*, I'd seen *Star Wars*. I didn't know that my character had already appeared in *The Empire Strikes Back*, so I went to watch that scene in which he appears in a hologram. That's not me, nor is it my voice—it's Clive Revill's.

How much did you work off of that scene?

Well, they gave me a tape to look at, and Richard said, "You shouldn't be too dissimilar vocally." I know Clive Revill's voice, so I knew it was a low resonant voice, but I reckon that's what I would have wanted to use anyway. As things went on, and also I saw the makeup and saw myself in the mirror and sort of got to know him a little bit better, this voice just came.

It's quite a voice.

It's considerably lower than my own, and sharper. But once again, when you're looking

Now I have an opportunity to play *myself younger than my own years, which has never happened to me before. So I suppose I'm getting to know this guy retrospectively.*

It was very cool, because the cloak itself was quite warm, so I was grateful for that. That was it, I'm afraid—nothing outrageous.

Another question that's gnawed at me—is it Palp-a-TEEN or Palp-a-TINE?

Well, I don't know. I don't think George has an absolute view on that either. I think in the end we came down in favor of Palp-a-TINE.

Were you there for the entire three months of Episode I's principal photography?

Yes, but I didn't get to go to Tunisia or Naples. I wasn't too disappointed not to go to Tunisia because it was extremely hot and I think people suffered a lot from the heat. But Naples sounded fun.

I must say, there are always problems and difficulties, but as far as I could judge, there were never any insurmountable ones. It was hard, and it was tough on absolutely everybody. It was a short schedule, and quite a punishing one, obviously for some more than others. But I think it was also characterized by the notion that we were involved in the continuation of a journey.

A lot of us used to have to pinch ourselves to remind ourselves what we were involved in. Ewan [McGregor], every now and again he'd be holding a lightsaber—"Hey, I'm holding a lightsaber!" Took him back to when he was a kid, I think.

I was lucky to be involved on the first day of shooting and the last. When we decided to go for the first shot of Number One after all those years, it was quite an emotional moment. There was a degree of anticipation and tension inevitably on the set. The air was full with a kind of expectancy, and we were all nervous. This was, after all, a historic moment.

What was the mood on the final day of shooting?

I was in the second to last shot, though I didn't manage to get in the last shot. That involved an exploding device of some kind. And George with typical showman's instinct, waited, did the shot from various angles, and in various ways, but waited for the final moment to press the special effects. So it finished with a light show and a bit of a bang. I thought that was a good showman's touch.

How much did you work with George Lucas on *Jedi*?

We just sort of met, and he did do the final sequence, when the Emperor is being sent down that chute—I won't say killed, because we don't know that, do we?

Lucas directed that scene?

Yes. It was principally for technical reasons. I was on a flying harness, and I had to be lifted at certain moments, and Richard was off doing other scenes with the second unit.

That was you, not a stuntman, being lifted in the air by David Prowse?

Yes, that was me. I was on a big hoist. All he had to do was catch my feet, which he did occasionally, to stop me from spinning around the studio. There was a lot of technical work, so George took that on himself. I just got to know him a little bit during that. But I hadn't seen him for 15 years when we met next, just before he decided that I should play the part once again—because it was by no means a foregone conclusion. Of course, I hoped it would be.

You didn't know if you'd get the part for the prequel?

There were no foregone conclusions about the film at all. I think George doesn't deal in foregone conclusions—which is fair enough. The technology is so advanced, none of us were quite sure how many of the characters would be human and how many would be digitally created. But I think that the humanity count on George Lucas films will always be very high indeed.

mperor meets with Darth Vader on the Death Star.

There were no foregone conclusions about the film [Episode 1] at all. I think George [Lucas] doesn't deal in foregone conclusions.

So what was the process? Did you have to audition?

It was almost the same as before. It was very nice to see him after 15 years, and we chatted for about 10 minutes, and that was it really. After that, it was costumes and makeup tests, and then I was shooting.

Had you already seen the Special Edition of *Return of the Jedi* at that point?

Oh, yes. I couldn't wait. I could see the little improvements, but by and large they haven't changed. And that's what's so interesting about the whole phenomenon of the Special Edition. New generations have responded to the film even more enthusiastically than our younger selves did. And that needn't have been the case. People could have said, "Oh, that's how they did it then, now we're so sophis-

ticated," you know, the GameBoy age and so on. And that's a great tribute to the power of these films, and also to George.

It's very much his vision. And it's not calculated, it's just an instinct he has about how to tell a story. It's the battle of good and evil—which has all the best lines and most of the best tunes, but which can't win because it's ultimately a negative force about death and not life. I've played quite a number of dark characters, and if you're going to play a villain in a movie, they don't come darker or more villainous than the Emperor ended up being.

Your scenes in *Return of the Jedi* are considered by many to have some of the strongest acting in the original *Star Wars* trilogy.

There's a lot of, I think, rather unfair comments about the acting in the *Star Wars* films. I

enjoyed those scenes very much — but I enjoyed the scenes because I was working with a very fine actor, Mark Hamill. We were in front of the camera for all of 10 days shooting, and Mark was giving 100 percent, and I hope I was giving the same back. Acting doesn't happen in a vacuum, you know—it's between two people.

Mark always had a wonderful sense of humor, so we were able to laugh between takes. It was enormous fun working with him, because he was extremely good, and also we could laugh—although when I laughed it hurt because of the makeup.

How long did it take to apply all that makeup for *Return of the Jedi*?

It started off at four hours. I used to go in at half past 3 in the morning. But [*Jedi* makeup artist] Nick Dudman, who's now in charge of creature effects in Episode I, did my makeup [for *Jedi*] quite superbly. I watched the Emperor take shape, slowly, over those four hours. He was so good at it, though, that by the third day he said, "The best thing you can do is go to sleep." There was very little that he needed me to do. In fact, a relaxed face was what he wanted. I went to sleep

>> Ian McDiarmid in a still from *Return of the Jedi* where he portrayed Emperor Palpatine.

as me and woke up as the Emperor.

That must have been a rude awakening. You must have seen a lot of characters pass through that makeup room.

One day, I was in for my four-hour makeup and I saw Sebastian Shaw [Anakin Skywalker in *Return of the Jedi*] in the corridor. I knew Sebastian quite well. I said, "Sebastian, good heavens, what are you doing here?" He said, "I don't know, dear boy, I think it's something to do with science-fiction."

That was Sebastian. The *Star Wars* saga had passed him blissfully by. So I think that's going to be my answer from now on—"I think it's something to do with science-fiction."

How different was your experience making Episode I from your memories of *Return of the Jedi*?

For *Jedi*, it was a straight block of shooting those scenes. There was the entry, and then everything else was in the throne room. It was contained and it was straight through, whereas here there were many scenes and different locations—even though most of them were against a blue screen background. We know it's going to look wonderful, but we've no real idea of what it will look like. I suppose when I go along and do any revoicing that has to be done, I'll get an impression then. But except George and the editors, no one will really see it until that first showing.

One of the reasons I think that they wanted to use Leavesden Studios [for the prequels] is because it could offer enormous acreage and huge spaces. But most of those huge spaces had aspects of the set—sometimes

quite detailed ones, sometimes hardly any, and you'd know that they'd always be filled in later.

But then we had exterior scenes. Again, they were on the backlot, and it looked like you'd imagine a great D.W. Griffith movie should look like—steps and columns and so on. I very naïvely asked George, "Why have you come outside to do this?" And he said, "Well, it's an external scene." A perfectly straightforward explanation! The blue screen on that was very well painted—God was shining favorably. There was a very beautiful blue in the sky, and not too many clouds, so I imagine Industrial Light & Magic got what they wanted.

Was there much rehearsal for the prequel?

We had a read-through, which the documentary crew documented. So I'm sure in years to come you'll see bits of that. But Liam [Neeson] was still filming in Prague at the time, so he couldn't be there. George rehearsed with Natalie [Portman] and me, but this was really so we could get to know each other a little better before we were plunged in and she, particularly, would be transformed by makeup, and there wouldn't be any time.

Do you have your Emperor action figure?

Every now and again somebody gives me one. Our company manager was in New York lately, and he brought back a fascinating little one that actually does shoot those thunderbolts. When I see it I think, 'God, I wish I had just a little bit of that in my pinky every now and again. I wouldn't hurt anybody, but it would be nice.' >>

>> "Oh... I'm afraid the deflector shield will be quite operational when your friends arrive."

You were a drama school classmate of Denis Lawson. Some people might be surprised to know that the Emperor and Wedge used to hang out together.

Yes indeed! We go back quite a long way. It was the Royal Scottish Academy of Dramatic Arts in Glasgow, and Denis and I were in the same year, though I think to be fair to... Wedge... he's a little bit younger than me, but not much. We were and still are very good friends. We used to make each other laugh a lot.

Were you disappointed you didn't have any scenes together in *Return of the Jedi*?

Yes, we were disappointed, but not surprised. There were a lot of people I knew in that film. One of the other pilots was a Scottish actor called Hilton McRae, and there were a few others, I can't remember who they all were. But of course the film was being made over here, and George liking British actors as much as he likes British technicians, that was inevitable.

You didn't do any *Jedi* scenes with Denis Lawson, but now you've worked with his nephew, Ewan McGregor, who plays the young Obi-Wan Kenobi in Episode I.

That's an even bigger coincidence!

Had you met Ewan when he was growing up?

I met Ewan when he came along to see his uncle and me in a play that we did together, Volpone, by Ben Jonson. It wasn't that long ago. He was still in drama school. And like everybody else, I've been delighted to watch his meteoric rise.

When in your life did you discover you were an actor?

Probably when I knew what it actually was to be an actor. I didn't come from a background where that kind of thing was readily encouraged. But I knew there was something inside me, and I learned later on to describe it as this thing called acting. That happened fairly early on, but I only had the courage to admit it after I'd left university and decided I should set about doing something I really wanted to do. Otherwise I'd be in a state of regret for the rest of my life.

Tell me about your theatre, the Almeida.

It's a small theatre in North London, but it's an unusual space. It has a very big stage area but the auditorium is very small, it seats 300 people. So you have something that's rare—a stage space of epic size, and an intimate auditorium. And that can make for the most electrifying experience.

We're trying to raise the money to expand to another theatre, because we all need new challenges. We've been to Broadway with Ralph Fiennes in *Hamlet*, and Diana Rigg in *Medea*. Now we have David Hare, who's a terrific writer. His new play is about Oscar Wilde, and we hope very much that will play Broadway as well. The leading role is going to be played by Liam Neeson, so there's another connection.

Much like George Lucas, you oversee a bustling creative enterprise. Do your duties as joint-artistic director keep you from acting?

I act in quite a lot of the plays here. I'm going to start rehearsals for a play on Monday. It's Gogol's *The Government Inspector*, probably Russia's greatest comedy—spiraling madness. It's a nice relief: even apart from *Star Wars*, I've played a spate of monsters lately.

You've played other villains recently?

Yes, I tend to. We did an opera here. No, I don't sing. It was an opera for actors rather than singers, based on Artaud's *The Cenci*. I was doing that at the same time as the filming down at Leavesden, and everybody was very good about coordinating the schedules so I could do both.

So you would do *Star Wars* during the day and opera at night?

Yes, it was hectic. But the great thing is they were only 40 minutes apart—it's 40 minutes to the center of the universe! It seemed so extraordinary to get up every morning and go to the Galactic Empire just down the road. It's very convenient.

I don't know if you know the story [of the opera] or not, but he's a complete monster, declares himself a monster, murders his son, and rapes his daughter. So the dark side was being well and truly investigated over the summer months.

Speaking of the Force, you were directed in *Dirty Rotten Scoundrels* by Frank Oz, who played Yoda. Looks like the Emperor was submitting to Yoda's will on that set.

Absolutely, yes. It was a very pleasurable submission, let me tell you. Frank is great to work with. He's enormous fun, very entertaining. Very good, very funny, very fastidious.

Had you met him on the set of *Return of the Jedi*?

I only met Frank when I went up for *Dirty Rotten Scoundrels* [five years later]. He said, "Would you mind improvising a little bit?" And I thought, 'No I don't, it's Frank Oz,' and he said, "I'll be Steve [Martin]." So we had about 45 minutes where we just sort of reeled about and laughed. And he gave me the part.

Did you cross paths with him on the set of the prequel?

Yes, I did. I was on-set one day when Yoda was, and Frank was there. It was very nice to see him, the same as ever. And I was happy to see that Yoda was still very much Frank's creature and didn't belong to computer technology.

But you didn't have any scenes together?

No, unfortunately. I suppose if there was going to be a meeting, it would be a dramatic one.

To say the least. Along those lines, you played Indiana Jones' uncle on *Young Indiana Jones*? Did that make you Sean Connery's brother?

I don't know, I don't think I was his uncle. I think I was a friend of his uncle's. I was a professor with him. But I read that too, that I was his uncle. Once again, the fans probably know much more about it than I do. I wouldn't want to contradict them.

Do you have any other films coming up?

None yet. I'm very happy to wait and see if the phone's going to ring and I'm going to be asked to be in Two and Three.

You don't know yet if you're in the next two *Star Wars* movies?

Well, I haven't been officially contracted, but I think it looks likely. I would like to think they were my next two. That would be very nice. But there are no certainties out there in the galactic universe.

ON YOUR TRAIL!
CREATING THE BOUNTY HUNTERS

ROMANCING A JEDI!
SATINE'S STORY REVEALED

STAR WARS
INSIDER

THE RETURN OF
BOBA FETT
READY FOR REVENGE!

ISSUE #117
MAY/JUNE 2010
U.S. $5.99 CAN $6.99

PETER SERAFINOWICZ
THE VOICE OF DARTH MAUL

ISSUE 117
MAY/JUNE 2010

As with Darth Vader, it took two actors to do justice to Darth Maul's body and voice! While Ray Park provided the finely tuned physique to play the character, it fell to Peter Serafinowicz to deliver the distinctive vocals that brought Maul to life. Though Serafinowicz has only a few lines in the film, his measured, darker-than-dark tones make them some of the most memorable!

Best known for assorted comedy roles, the actor is as witty as you might expect, and a very enthusiastic *Star Wars* fan. He is also a lifelong friend of Lewis McLeod, who played Sebulba in *The Phantom Menace*. It is amusing to think of the excitement the two young actors must have felt on learning they were both playing key roles in a new *Star Wars* movie back in the 1990s!—Jonathan Wilkins

Peter Szymon Serafinowicz *was born July 10, 1972. A man of many talents, he is an actor, comedian, writer, and voice artist. Serafinowicz played Pete in* Shaun of the Dead *(2004) and Denarian Garthan Saal in* Guardians of the Galaxy *(2014). He has also appeared in numerous comedy programmes in the U.S. and U.K., including* Parks and Recreation.

MY STAR WARS

PETER SERAFINOWICZ'S CAREER AS A COMEDY ACTOR (YOU MIGHT REMEMBER HIM FROM *SHAUN OF THE DEAD* AND HE'S SOON TO PLAY PAUL MCCARTNEY IN THE *YELLOW SUBMARINE* REMAKE) TOOK AN UNEXPECTED TWIST IN THE LATE 1990S WHEN HE VOICED THE PIVOTAL CHARACTER OF DARTH MAUL IN *STAR WARS: EPISODE I THE PHANTOM MENACE*. IT PROVED TO BE A DREAM JOB FOR THIS LIFELONG FAN OF THE SAGA! WORDS: JONATHAN WILKINS

When did you become a *Star Wars* fan?
It wasn't until it was on TV that it really clicked. We recorded it from TV when I was about 10 or 11. I watched it with my brother James every day, and sometimes we watched it twice in one day, so it's embedded in my psyche. Now it's my favorite film! It's so imaginative, and huge. Some people say that *The Empire Strikes Back* is the best film, but for me *Star Wars*, the first one, is the best; the original and the best!

What was your first *Star Wars* experience?
Well, it was *Star Wars*, the first one, which, of course, is *A New Hope*. My mum took me to see it when I was five after I'd begged. When I got to the cinema, after about 20 minutes I was saying, "Please, I'm so bored, why did you take me here? I hate it!"

Do you have any Darth Maul toys?
I've got one that doesn't have my voice on it! It has a sort of computer pretending to be my voice. It says, [in a computer sounding Darth Maul voice] "At last we will reveal ourselves to the Jedi. At last we will have revenge." That's quite a post-modern thing, to be impersonated by a computer speech synthesizer. It is strange.

What is your happiest memory about being in *The Phantom Menace*?
I love Ian McDiarmid, who I got to meet recently in a café. I went up to him and introduced myself. I said, "Look, we've actually worked together although we've never met!" He's a giant in acting, and his voice is just something else. He's got such command over his voice. I feel like I've stolen so many tricks and techniques from him. Also, my really good friend, Lewis MacLeod, did the voice for Sebulba, and I loved his character.

Can you tell us a previously unknown nugget of information about you?
Not a lot of people know that I did a few different voices in *The Phantom Menace*! Not only did I do Darth Maul, I also voiced the battle droid that confronts Qui-Gon and Obi-Wan and says, "Let me see your identification." Also, there's one scene where the action cuts from Darth Maul saying, "Yes, my master," to a Gungan saying, "They's a-coming!" That goes from me to me in the same film, and I'm playing two different characters! Surely that's the first and only time that's happened in *Star Wars*?

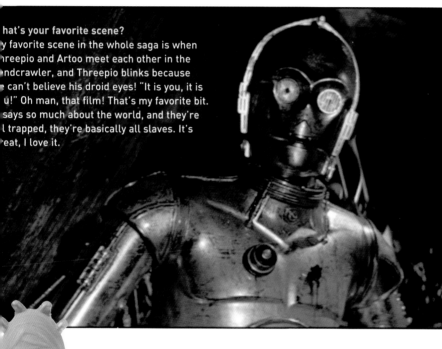

hat's your favorite scene?
y favorite scene in the whole saga is when hreepio and Artoo meet each other in the ndcrawler, and Threepio blinks because e can't believe his droid eyes! "It is you, it is u!" Oh man, that film! That's my favorite bit. says so much about the world, and they're l trapped, they're basically all slaves. It's eat, I love it.

Did you have a favorite *Star Wars* toy as a child?
I had one *Star Wars* toy as a kid. I had a Sand Person. Later on he was joined by a second-hand C-3PO and R2-D2, and that was it!

What do you think gives *Star Wars* such longevity?
Part of the reason *Star Wars* is so great is the cast of characters. The action figures cemented that in a way. Take Hammerhead: He's an alien in the cantina for one shot in the movie, but he has his own action figure and identity. These minor characters from the film had their own life. Boba Fett is in the original trilogy for a few brief scenes, and yet he's got something about him that people love.

EXPANDED UNIVERSE
www.peterserafinowicz.com

ASKING ANAKIN
MATT LANTER INTERVIEWED !

EVIL DEEDS
STAR WARS' DARKEST MOMENTS

THE OLD REPUBLIC
WE PREVIEW THE GAME THAT WILL BLOW YOUR MIND!

VILLAINS
V
SPECIAL

STAR WARS

EXCLUSIVE INTERVIEW!

THE CLONE WARS PRODUCER CARY SILVER ON SEASON TWO

JOIN US!
THE VILLAINS OF STAR WARS

KILL KENOBI!
HOW THE FORCE UNLEASHED:
ULTIMATE SITH EDITION
IS REWRITING HISTORY!

STAR WARS INSIDER
#113   Dec 2009
US $7.99 CAN $9.99

COUNT DOOKU
THE FALLEN JEDI

ISSUE 113
DECEMBER 2009

Played with great distinction by Sir Christopher Lee, Count Dooku is a wonderfully enigmatic figure first introduced in Episode II: *Attack of the Clones*. A former Jedi turned-rebel-turned-Sith made for an intriguing character who could hold his own verbally against Obi-Wan Kenobi and physically in a show-stopping duel with Master Yoda. As the character has developed—with appearances in *Revenge of the Sith* and *Star Wars: The Clone Wars*—we've slowly learned more about him, but without dispelling all the mystery that keeps us hoping there is still more to come...**—Jonathan Wilkins**

COUNT DOOKU

By Daniel Wallace

"The democratic process in the Republic is a sham. The time will come when that cult of greed called the Republic will lose even the pretext of democracy and freedom."
—**Count Dooku to Senator Padmé Amidala**

Dooku was in his 80s at the time of his death, a distinguished silver-haired elder statesman. This was the image he projected to the galaxy, one that allowed him to recruit new members into his Separatist movement. Dooku's heart was cold and remote, and his willingness to orchestrate the Clone Wars invalidated every good deed he had achieved as a Jedi. Dooku carried a lightsaber with a curved handle and practiced an elegant fencing style; he could outclass nearly any opponent except for Yoda.

Dooku was a unique case in the history of the Jedi Order. Universally respected, he would have been a Master on a par with Yoda had he not abandoned the Order to join its greatest enemies. A study in contradiction, he was a Sith Lord with a bust of honor in the Jedi Archives, and a Clone Wars criminal who was widely considered a man of peace.

Unlike most younglings brought up inside Coruscant's Jedi Temple, Dooku knew of his birthright as heir to a noble family of Serenno. The belief that he was better than the other students only seemed to gain further validation when Dooku demonstrated an understanding of the Force far beyond that of his peers. Yoda recognized Dooku's potential and spent much time instructing him in the arts of telekinesis and lightsaber combat. Naturally standoffish, Dooku did not make friends easily, a trait exacerbated when his fellow student Lorian Nod stole a Sith holocron and tried to pin the blame on Dooku. The Jedi Council expelled Nod when the truth came out, but Dooku became convinced that close relationships always ended in betrayal.

JEDI HERO?

In adolescence Dooku became the Padawan learner of Thame Cerulian, a Jedi scholar on the Council who called Dooku the finest swordsman he had ever seen. In short order Dooku passed the trials of Knighthood, then took on his own apprentice, Qui-Gon Jinn. Though they made an effective team, Dooku couldn't understand his Padawan's reckless attachment to "lesser life forms." Following Qui-Gon's graduation to the rank of Jedi Knight, Dooku selected Komari Vosa as his second Padawan.

Throughout his tenure as a Jedi, Dooku studied history and politics, intrigued by the responsibility the Jedi held for upholding the Republic's institutions. Yet he could not ignore the fact that Coruscant politicians were a lazy and greedy bunch, freely taking bribes and remaining deaf to public calls for reform. That the Jedi would so readily defend a corrupt institution disturbed him. Eventually Komari Vosa disappeared on a mission, but Dooku was not troubled, for he and his Padawan had never been close. Far more disturbing was the news that Qui-Gon Jinn had been killed on Naboo at the hands of a Sith assassin. Dooku shocked the Council by choosing that moment to resign from the Jedi Order. The Council claimed to respect his decision, and enshrined Dooku alongside other famous principled objectors as the Lost Twenty.

"Become unreliable Dooku has. Joined the dark side. Lies, deceit, creating mistrust are his ways now."
—Jedi Master Yoda

BIRTHRIGHT

Dooku returned to Serenno to take up his birthright as count. He also made an alliance with Darth Sidious. Though Sidious had been behind the death of Qui-Gon Jinn, Dooku understood the bigger picture and realized that only the Sith had a hope of restructuring the galaxy. Dooku became Sidious' new apprentice, and accepted the Sith title Darth Tyranus.

Because Sidious held official power in his alternate identity of Supreme Chancellor

Palpatine, the path to revolution became clear. Dooku murdered his former Jedi colleague Sifo-Dyas and took charge of a clone army that Sifo-Dyas had ordered from the geneticists of Kamino. To supply the template for the army, Dooku selected Jango Fett after the Mandalorian proved his worth by killing Dooku's rogue Padawan Komari Vosa.

At the same time, Dooku set about building a second army at the droid factories of Geonosis. With Palpatine leading the clones and Dooku commanding the droids, the two Sith Lords could manufacture a false war with the Jedi caught in the middle.

Their plan worked better than Dooku had imagined. Giving speeches and appealing to decades-old frustrations, Dooku persuaded thousands of star systems to secede. His Separatist movement took formal shape as the Confederacy of Independent Systems, with the Trade Federation, Commerce Guild, and other mercantile powers signing on. After Obi-Wan Kenobi uncovered the clone army and the Republic Senate gave Palpatine the authority to use it, the two sides clashed in the Battle of Geonosis. Dooku cut off Anakin Skywalker's arm in a lightsaber fight, but fled when Yoda threatened to overwhelm him.

Over the next three years, Count Dooku ordered his armies into fights that devastated worlds. He relied on the loyal service of his agents Asajj Ventress and General Grievous, and enlisted the likes of Lok Durd and Pre Vizsla of Death Watch

to fight for the Separatist cause. Anakin Skywalker proved to be the cause of most of Dooku's setbacks, as when he and his Padawan Ahsoka Tano exposed the plot to kidnap Jabba the Hutt's offspring. But Dooku had beaten Anakin once, and had no doubt that he could beat him again. His arrogance proved to be his doom. In orbit above Coruscant during the final battle of the Clone Wars, Dooku faced off against Skywalker with Palpatine as a witness. Skywalker, whose skills had deepened over years of warfare, chopped off Dooku's hands and prepared to remove his head. A single command from Palpatine—"Kill him!"—was all it took. Dooku lay dead, a casualty of the Sith Rule of Two. ☪

"Your moves are clumsy Kenobi... too predictable. You'll have to do better."
—Count Dooku

ALL NEW!

STAR WARS®
INSIDER

ISSUE 80

CLONE WARS
SEASON 2

**EXCLUSIVE INTERVIEW WITH
GENNDY TARTAKOVSKY AND
PAUL RUDISH**

EPISODE III UPDATE
EXCLUSIVE PHOTOS

JEDI vs. SITH
SAMUEL L. JACKSON AND
CHRISTOPHER LEE INTERVIEWS

MANDALORIAN 101
HISTORY OF THE GALAXY'S
GREATEST WARRIORS

U.S. $5.99/Canada $8.99

BANTHA TRACKS *STAR WARS* FAN ART FROM AROUND THE GALAXY

EXCLUSIVE ONLINE CONTENT!
- ALL-NEW EPISODE III SET SNAPS
- MAKING MAGIC AT ILM
- RARE AND NEVER-SEEN-BEFORE PHOTOS

starwars.com

AN IDG COMMUNICATIONS PUBLICATION

THE MAGAZINE OF HYPERSPACE: THE OFFICIAL STAR WARS FAN CLUB

FICTION • BOOKS • COMICS • TOYS • GAMING • FANDOM • MOVIES • COLLECTIBLES • SHOP

CHRISTOPHER LEE
DARTH TYRANUS

ISSUE 51
JANUARY 2005

THIS MONTH, FAR, FAR AWAY....

Labyrinth of Evil published

Has there been a greater source of movie villainy than Christopher Lee? From *Dracula* (1958) to *The Hobbit* (2014), via *The Man with the Golden Gun* (1974) and many others, he menaced cinemagoers for decades. It seemed only right, therefore, that he would eventually appear in *Star Wars*. He is the kind of actor that fits perfectly into the *Star Wars* universe, following on from his close friend and fellow Hammer alumnus Peter Cushing as a kind of elder statesman of cinema. This interview, by former *Insider* editor-in-chief Brett Rector, finds Lee making his *Star Wars* debut at the tender age of 80!
—Jonathan Wilkins

Sir Christopher Frank Carandini Lee, CBE, CStJ, was born in London on May 27, 1922. An actor, singer, and author, he was best known throughout his 70-year career for portraying villains—most famously Count Dracula in several Hammer horror films. Aside from Star Wars, *his other notable roles include Lord Summerisle in* The Wicker Man *(1973), Francisco Scaramanga in the James Bond movie* The Man with the Golden Gun *(1974), and Saruman in* The Lord of the Rings *trilogy (2001–2003) and* The Hobbit *trilogy (2012–2014). He died shortly after his 93rd birthday on June 7, 2015.*

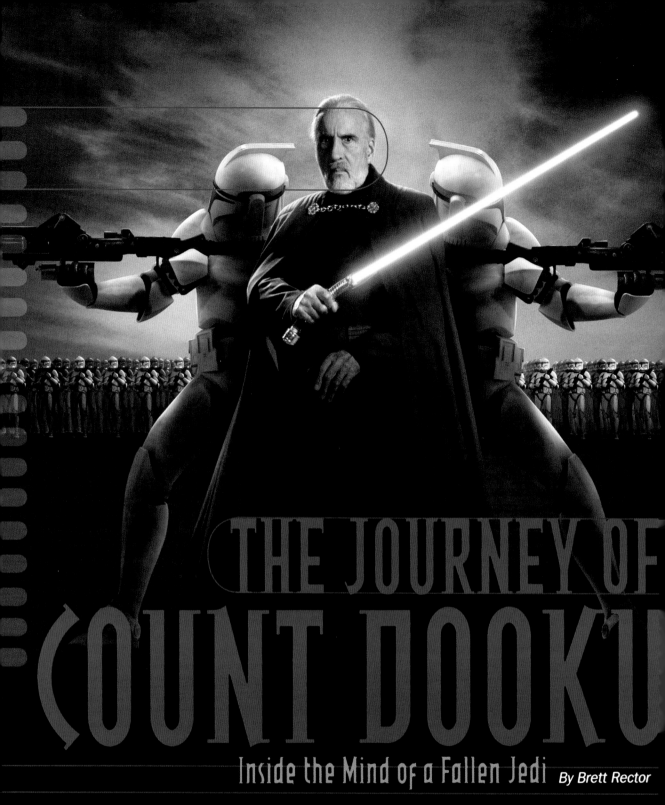

THE JOURNEY OF COUNT DOOKU

Inside the Mind of a Fallen Jedi
By Brett Rector

He is the actor of a thousand faces. and his illustrious career is well into its eighth decade. He has worked with some of the world's most well-known actors. and he has shared the stage with hundreds more. He may have gone toe to toe with Errol Flynn. but he will be most remembered for his epic confrontation with Yoda. He perfected the art of playing the villain. yet his demeanor is anything but villainous. He is. by all

hristopher Lee will go down in cinematic history as one of the most prolific actors that ever lived. However, now is not the time to wax philosophical about the man who breathed life into Count Dracula but rather to delve into the mind of the man who portrays Count Dooku. Recently, the soft-spoken actor gave his views on George Lucas, the story at large, and the corruption of the Jedi.

Now that you've played the character in two movies what do you find fascinating about Count Dooku?

For one, his name, which means "poison" in Japanese. Something I'm sure George probably knew. It's a very appropriate name because he's very lethal. The character himself is fascinating in many respects because he's a Jedi, one of what they call the Last 20. Just playing a Jedi in and of itself is a unique experience, I would say, for any actor because very few are alive in the *Star Wars* world at the time. Dooku is also an antagonist—a Sith Lord. And there aren't many of them either. Being a Sith suggests that he has immense powers, both physical and mental, and that he's unstoppable.

During your career, you've dabbled a little bit in science fiction, although Star Wars *is more science fantasy . But has anything really come close to this?*

Many years ago, I appeared in one of the very first science-fiction television shows, *Space 1999*, opposite Martin Landau. But no, I've never done anything like this.

with each successive year, something incredible seems to happen, and technologically, you find things that make it easier for people to produce these amazing effects. When doing a film, I read the script so I know what the scene is about and I know what I'm supposed to be doing—but I don't know what it's going to look like behind, in front of, below, and above me until I see the film. And it really is mind-boggling how the (special) effects are implemented.

Because to know would be like peeking behind a magician's curtain?

It is magic, and magic can be created in many ways. It's like a magician who stands in front of an audience and says, "Look, nothing up this sleeve, nothing up that sleeve. Now, come with me into my magical world." The audience has no idea, except for perhaps a few specialists, how the effects are actually done. I don't want to know how it's done because I want the experience to be pure.

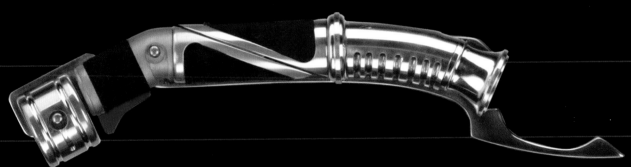

The time frame is a little bit more far reaching as well, even more so than The Lord of the Rings*?*

I was talking with George recently about the time frame when all the events in the prequels are supposed to be happening, and he said *Star Wars* is millions of years old. *The Lord of the Rings* was only supposed to take place a mere 7,000 years ago in Middle-earth, which as far as Tolkein was concerned was somewhere near Oxford in the countryside.

The movies you've recently starred in have been very CGI intensive. What has been your experience working primarily in front of bluescreen?

I have actually done a lot of bluescreen work in my life. I've also done greenscreen and even yellowscreen at Disney. It's really all the same. But

Did you work in front of a bluescreen in the Lord of the Rings *films as much as you did so for Episode II and III?*

For *The Lord of the Rings*, there was a certain amount of bluescreen work to be done but nothing like this. When I saw those films, I never thought that what I was seeing was special effects—I believed it implicitly. Just as it got to the point where I didn't think of the performers as being actors and actresses dressed up playing parts, I believed them to be real people. I can also suspend this belief—or if you like, disbelief—while watching *Star Wars*. The people become real. And to the audience, they should be. After all, *Star Wars* is the ultimate in filmmaking and film viewing for literally millions of people the world over.

And that really is the testament to George Lucas' overall vision for his films.

This has all come from his head. It's not from books or stories—he's done it. Even *The Lord of the Rings* films come from three books. During filming, I had some relatives visit me on set, of which there were three children. I explained to them, the best that I could, about all the cameras, monitors, and things that were around, and they were completely bowled over.

What have you noticed about Ewan McGregor and Hayden Christensen as you've worked with them over the course of the two films

It's been fascinating for me because I can see within minutes if they really care about what they're doing, if they really want to make it believable, and if they are dedicated to what they're doing and devoted to their craft. Ewan

"...Dooku makes the switch of his own accord-nobody makes him do it, no one suggests that he do it, which is different from Anakin."

has already done quite a few major films and starred in different roles. He's had a lot of good fortune. What I noticed about him is he is completely involved with everything he does—he goes straight into projects and becomes completely dedicated. That's what [acting] is all about: dedication and devotion to what you're doing. You also have to have powers of invention, you have to be imaginative, and you have to have the right instincts.

Hayden is at the beginning of his career, and when I spoke to him recently, we were talking about what an actor does these days. I told him to forget about being rich and famous and concentrate on making your own decisions (about future projects). He knows that [the Star Wars] films are going to make him a big name and grant him a huge following. And for a while, he knows he's going to have to live with the fact that he will be known for his role as Anakin Skywalker/Darth Vader. But I told him he's a good enough actor and that he cares enough to learn to play other roles.

Both Count Dooku and Anakin are Jedi who have or will convert to the Stith. How does Anakin's conversion differ from Dooku's

[Dooku] crossed over for personal reasons and became a Separatist because he was disgusted with the way the Republic was functioning. But Dooku makes the switch on his own accord—nobody makes him do it, no one suggests that he do it, which is different from Anakin. He does so without knowing it or even wanting it and becomes enmeshed in a trap by the Emperor

The corruption of Anakin is uitimate goal, and the approach is very Shakespearean

In many ways [the Star Wars saga] is like a Shakespearean tragedy. It's also the same with Tolkein and The Lord of the Rings. Don't forget that, eventually, good triumphs over evil in the end, and it follows the same course here at the conclusion of Return of the Jedi.

Ther's also that lust for power

Yes, and it initially emanates from the Emperor, who is also very corrupt himself. What was he like when he was a young man? Who knows? Because not many people are corrupt from the moment they're born—it does take time.

Would you say that, like the Emperor, Count Dooku is an evil character—a dad guy

No, he's not simply a bad guy. He was good and then becomes bad. At or time, Dooku was a decent and good man. He obviously holds very stron beliefs. And maybe at one time he was right—maybe the Republic was co rupt and he decided he didn't want to become corrupt himself. So he saic "I'm going over here and I'm going to start my own group." Then, of cours it becomes a war, which is another matter altogether. Everyone has a darl side—everyone. The important thing is to make sure the dark side doesn overpower the light side. ☯

STAR WARS

THE DARK SIDE TRIUMPHANT!

THE EVIL PLANS OF SAVAGE OPRESS AND THE NIGHTSISTERS REVEALED!

ISSUE #122
JANUARY
U.S. $7.99
CAN $9.99

TITAN

ASAJJ VENTRESS
NIKA FUTTERMAN

ISSUE 122
JANUARY 2011

The Oscar-winning sound designer and *Star Wars: The Clone Wars* director Walter Murch once sang the praises of Assaj Ventress. Speaking to *Insider* back in 2012, he said: "She's a fantastic character. I love how she is animated." It's very hard to disagree. Much like Ahsoka Tano, Ventress is a character you could easily believe has been a part of the *Star Wars* saga from the start. She feels as established as Obi-Wan Kenobi and General Grievous, and her appearances in *The Clone Wars* were always highlights. Despite her evil deeds, we felt sympathy when we learned her sad backstory, and enjoyed the light and shade she was afforded throughout her arc. Much of the credit for this memorable character must go to Nika Futterman, the actor who brought her to life in 14 episodes of the show.—**Jonathan Wilkins**

Nika Futterman was born on October 25, 1969 and is an actor, comedian and singer. She has voiced numerous animated characters, including Catwoman in Batman: The Brave and the Bold *(2008–2011) and Gridface Princess in* Adventure Time *(2010–), and also sang the line "Give it to me baby," in The Offspring's 1998 hit, "Pretty Fly for a White Guy."*

THE
S

SULTRY SITH

CUNNING, DEVIOUS, AND MORE POWERFUL WITH THE FORCE THAN HER SITH MASTERS COULD HAVE FORESEEN, ASAJJ VENTRESS' TIME HAS COME WITH AN EPIC STORYLINE IN *STAR WARS: THE CLONE WARS. INSIDER* EXPLORES THE ORIGINS OF THIS INFAMOUS *STAR WARS* CHARACTER, AND MEETS THE ACTRESS BEHIND HER LATEST INCARNATION. WORDS: JONATHAN WILKINS

ORIGINS OF ASAJJ VENTRESS

The distinctive look of Asajj Ventress came from early *Attack of the Clones* sketches by Dermot Power, who—along with concept artist Iain McCaig—explored a number of female Sith Lord concepts. As the script changed, this direction was abandoned and Christopher Lee was cast to fill the role of Darth Sidious' new apprentice, Count Dooku. McCaig and Power's concept sketches were filed and eventually used as the basis for a new villain that was needed for the *Clone Wars* micro-series in 2003.

The name Asajj was inspired by the character Asaji from Akira Kurosawa's *Throne of Blood*. Ventress originally was going to be named Juno Eclipse, but she underwent a name change to make her sound more villainous. The name Juno Eclipse was eventually given to the female co-star of *Star Wars: The Force Unleashed*.

Ventress was first voiced by Grey DeLisle in the 2003 *Star Wars: Clone Wars* micro-series. Actress Nika Futterman took on the role in the 2008 *Star Wars: The Clone Wars* movie and the subsequent TV show

WHO IS ASAJJ VENTRESS?

Although not officially a Sith apprentice, Ventress is well-trained in the Sith arts by her master, Count Dooku.

Alluring, cunning, and fiendishly clever, Ventress takes sadistic pleasure in tormenting her victims before killing them. Using her exotic magnetism, Ventress often distracts her foes before dispatching them.

She carries twin-curved lightsabers, given to her by Dooku, that connect to become a double-bladed weapon.

A flamboyant Force user, Ventress uses telekinesis and Force speed during combat, as well as the gravity-defying Force jump. Her skills with the dark side include the use of the Force grip, and the ability to control others' minds.

This page; Dermot Power's concept art that inspired the look of Asajj Ventress.

VOICING VENTRESS

Actress Nika Futterman has played the role of Asajj Ventress since 2008's *Star Wars: The Clone Wars* movie. "I just assumed she had a difficult childhood!" she tells Jonathan Wilkins and James Burns.

Asajj Ventress has grown even more powerful in the Sith arts since we last saw her. Have you approached playing her differently this time round?

Although she's back and more powerful, to me she is still the same person as she was before, and I'm playing her from the same place.

What are the challenges of playing Asajj Ventress?

I think the biggest challenge has been figuring out who she is. We didn't know a lot about her originally. The writers were creating her character as I was playing her, so I was coming from the same

place as the audience, and asking, *Who is she?* I didn't want to play her just as a one-note character, because she does have a big history, and I knew we would explore that further down the line.

Were you aware of her back-story?

I had no idea about her back-story. The progression of the series is top secret, even to the actors! I always felt very free playing her, even when I had no idea where she came from. I just assumed she had a difficult childhood, and that led to her feeling

> "I DON'T CONSIDER ASAJJ TO BE TRAGIC. I STILL BELIEVE SHE HAS A CHANCE TO MOVE TOWARD THE LIGHT."

that she needed to prove something. Powerful people tend to come from backgrounds where they are making up for things they never had, searching for power, because they've always felt powerless. Learning about her past only strengthened the direction in which I was already heading.

Nothing surprised me in the storyline, it just showed me my instincts were correct.

Is evil fun to play?
Evil is the most fun to play! For me, most of my work is for kids shows and it involves playing funny and happy characters—so evil is the complete opposite of what I usually do.

Asajj has an all-new look this season. What do you think of her new threads?
I had no idea she had a new look. Like everyone else, I was psyched she got a new outfit!

Do you feel that she's a tragic character in a way? She's essentially punished for being too good at what she does.

I don't consider Asajj to be tragic. I think if I played her with a sense of tragedy it would indicate there's no hope for her future. It would leave no sense of promise in her being. I still believe she has a chance of moving toward the light. She just needs to be given the chance. As for her being punished for being too good at what she does, you have to hate the game not the player! And she can certainly handle the haters!

Do you empathize with her at all?
I completely empathize with Asajj. She's basically walking the galaxy

OTHER FUTTERMAN FAVORITES!

Like many in the cast members, Nika Futterman also provides voices of other characters. Remember Shaeeah in "The Deserter," and Chi Eekway Papanoida and TC-7 in "Sphere of Influence?" They're all voiced by Nika Futterman!

alone, used, and misunderstood. She's lost all she ever cared about, and now the only thing that drives her is revenge. I think she's gotten to the point where she believes feelings mean weakness, and that's really sad.

Does she recognize the dark side in Anakin?

I haven't seen anything in the show yet that indicates her seeing Anakin's dark side, although at some point I know it will be impossible for her to not see it. Darkness sees darkness!

Would Ventress' actions make a formidable Sith Master?

Asajj is certainly capable of anything. Whether she curbs her anger is yet to be determined. Revenge can get in the way of anyone becoming a Master.

What's the most satisfying thing about playing Asajj Ventress?

It has to be her multiple layers. She could just be a kick-butt, sexy character, but she's also got a history and intelligence and most of all, shows no fear. Playing someone with nothing to lose leaves open endless possibilities. It's fun playing a part that I haven't fully figured out yet. This season is the first real exploration into why Ventress is the way she is, and it's really compelling!

What's the secret to being a great voice actor?

I think the great voice actors are the ones with the greatest imagination. Unlike being on camera, you actually have to imagine your environment. You also need to have a range where you can play somebody who's two or 92 years old, so listening to people and being able to imitate them is very important.

> "I THINK SHE'S GOT TO THE POINT WHERE SHE BELIEVES FEELINGS MEAN WEAKNESS, AND THAT'S VERY SAD."

Do you have a favorite piece of Ventress merchandise?

It's always incredibly exciting when one of my characters becomes an action figure! My favorite has to be my LEGO figure! That makes me feel like I've made it—the Asajj Ventress LEGO figure is just too cool!

Do you think Asajj could take down Ahsoka?

Oh yeah, definitely [laughs]! Asajj is very powerful, but Ahsoka's got so much heart, and she cares so much. I think it would be a great fight. We've seen some of it, and I think there has to be more. ☾

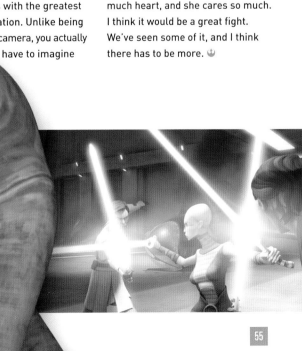

STAR WARS

INSIDER ®

ISSUE #159
U.S. $7.99
CAN $9.99
AUG/SEPT 2015

TITAN

ASAJJ VENTRESS
SITH APPRENTICE

ISSUE 159
AUGUST/SEPTEMBER 2015

In July 2015, Asajj Ventress starred in her own novel, Christie Golden's very well-received *Dark Disciple*. The book, part of *The Clone Wars* Legacy multimedia initiative, is based on a story arc originally intended for the *Star Wars: The Clone Wars* animated series. The unmade episodes, "Lethal Alliance," "The Mission," "Conspirators," "Dark Disciple," "Saving Vos Part I and II," "Traitor," and "The Path," were combined to form an epic tale featuring the troubled Sith acolyte. Who better than Tricia Barr to take an in-depth look at one of the key characters of *The Clone Wars*, and an evergreen fan favorite?—**Jonathan Wilkins**

THIS MONTH, FAR, FAR AWAY....

Kanan's Jedi Training released

Obsessed With Star Wars reissued in paperback

Lando, Part II released

Star Wars 8: Showdown on the Smuggler's Moon, Part I released

Revenge of the Sith: Episode III (LEGO *Star Wars*) released

Lando, Part III released

Disney Infinity 3.0 released

LEGO Star Wars: Free the Galaxy released

Star Wars Rebels: Complete Season One released on home formats

Stores around the world open at midnight to sell numerous products related to *Star Wars: The Force Awakens* for the first time on "Force Friday"

Star Wars: Aftermath released

ASAJJ VENTRESS
A-TYPICAL ANTI-HERO

TRICIA BARR CONTINUES HER ANALYSIS OF ICONIC *STAR WARS* CHARACTERS. THIS ISSUE, ONE OF THE SAGA'S MOST COMPLICATED VILLAINS.

Often heroes are born of ideas, grand notions of saviors. Heroes must face down villains, the opponents over whom the hero triumphs along their epic journey. Sometimes, though, a story focuses on the arc of a protagonist who lacks usual heroic traits like nobility and selflessness—an anti-hero. The simplest example is Anakin Skywalker's descent into darkness in *Revenge of the Sith*; he is no hero as that chapter of his saga concludes. Since his tragic story unfolded on screen, many more anti-heroes have followed in his wake. One of my favorites is assassin-turned-bounty hunter Asajj Ventress, whose path to greatness was far from typical.

When the *Ultimate Star Wars* writing assignments were distributed, I was excited to receive some of my favorite characters, including Princess Leia, Ahsoka Tano, and Asajj Ventress. Condensing characters like Leia and Luke Skywalker, while intimidating because of their importance to the saga, actually proved far simpler than the ladies from *Star Wars: The Clone Wars*. *Ultimate Star Wars* is intended to serve as a summary of the canon events from the movies and television shows. Within that scope, both Luke and Leia have relatively tight character arcs that play out over three movies. Summarizing Ahsoka proved easier than Asajj, even though Ventress did not have quite the catalogue of episode appearances. The sporadic nature of her unfolding arc created part of the challenge, but so did the fact that Asajj Ventress started as an idea in George Lucas's imagination long before she became a fascinating piece of *Clone Wars* lore.

SMALL BEGINNINGS

Star Wars has a long legacy of characters evolving from small beginnings to become impactful participants in the fabric of the saga. The most recognizable example is Boba Fett, who began to take on a life of his own with the release of his action-figure prior to the theatrical debut of *The Empire Strikes Back*. From there, the bounty hunter's tale is the stuff of legend, or rather spread across a vast portion of the Legends stories as well as playing a role in the prequel trilogy and *The Clone Wars* television show. Other background characters, such as Aurra Sing and Bossk, have earned more affection from fans than was originally imagined for them. Asajj Ventress's origin is even more humble than a character developed to populate the world-building; she started as a visual that did not make the original cut during the movie-making process.

Concept art for a menacing Sith warrior can be found in *The Art of Star Wars Episode II: Attack of the Clones*. Villainous women were championed by Iain McCaig, also known for his designs of Padmé and Queen Amidala. In the book, McCaig discusses the creation process for the *Attack of the Clones'* new Sith: "I felt this was a great opportunity to introduce a strong woman character, to give girl fans an icon." While McCaig experimented with female Sith variations like a Padmé-inspired dark queen and a medusa-like alien, Dermot Power developed a vampiric, shaven-headed warrior and martial arts-inspired alien with dual blades. This was not the first time a female villain had been tossed around in the conceptual phase; a fearsome Sith witch appeared in *The Phantom Menace* concept art. The Sith witch was set aside in favor of Darth Maul, and the female Sith warriors did not

make the cut for the second prequel movie, either. McCaig admits to being disappointed by the decision to move away from the female Sith conceptualization, but as with many good ideas in *Star Wars*, these striking designs would live to see another day.

Asajj Ventress was given a name when the artwork was fleshed out into a character (no longer a Sith) as part of the *Clone Wars* multi-media project from 2002-2005, which included the *Star Wars: Clone Wars* micro-series, books, and comics. It sought to tell stories within the timeline between *Attack of the Clones* and *Revenge of the Sith*, giving depth to the events that led to the fall of the Jedi Order and the rise of the Empire. The heroes of the Republic would face off with the conquering villains in Episode III, but as they moved toward their ultimate defeat, new foes were necessary to create surmountable obstacles, affording the heroes some victories along the way.

Clockwise from right: An attempted takedown of Count Dooku; the mysterious, alluring Ventress; Ventress battles Ahsoka Tano; proving a match for Anakin Skywalker.

"A COLD-HEARTED HARPY"

Not every character in *Star Wars* will experience an arc, but when characters are used over an extended number of stories across multiple mediums, arcs can emerge. Asajj Ventress was a compelling presence. She had an air of mystery and danger. She dueled Jedi standouts, Anakin Skywalker and Obi-Wan Kenobi with confidence, delivering biting banter. A female warrior fighting Jedi men hinted at chemistry similar to ill-fated relationships that have arisen over the centuries in literature. While professional creators bounced Obi-Wan or Anakin against Asajj like flint to rock, fandom took those sparks and fanned the flames. While Ventress created electricity in stories from Gendy Tartakovsky's *Clone Wars* to *Jedi Trial* and *Obsession*, her personal story consisted mostly of being an adversary.

Asajj Ventress's arc started to shine during the *Star Wars: The Clone Wars* television show when writer Katie Lucas developed a fondness for the character. In an interview with ComicBook.com discussing the second trilogy of episodes she wrote for the series, Lucas revealed, "I've really fallen for Ventress, and here the audience gets to learn a lot about her history. She's an extremely complicated character." Calling Ventress a "cold-hearted harpy," Lucas set out to create a story where she finally "owns herself." With her powers growing, Ventress becomes seen as a threat to Sidious's machinations and her mentor, Count Dooku, is ordered to kill her. Inspired by *Buffy the Vampire Slayer* and *Tank Girl*,

KATIE LUCAS SET OUT TO CREATE A STORY WHERE ASAJJ VENTRESS FINALLY "OWNS HERSELF."

GET TO KNOW ASAJJ VENTRESS

THE FORMER SITH ACOLYTE-TURNED-BOUNTY HUNTER PLAYS KEY ROLES IN SOME OF THE MOST EXCITING EPISODES OF *STAR WARS: THE CLONE WARS*. HERE IS WHERE YOU CAN FIND HER:

"The Hidden Enemy" (Season 1, episode 16) & *Star Wars: The Clone Wars* (movie) Asajj Ventress duels Obi-Wan Kenobi and Anakin Skywalker as she sets in motion the events leading to the Battle of Christophsis, then faces off with the two Jedi again after she has kidnapped Rotta the Huttlet in a plot to turn Jabba the Hutt's forces against the Republic.

"Ambush" (Season 1, episode 1) Ventress attempts to intimidate the Toydarian King Katunko from allying with the Republic, but her efforts are thwarted by Yoda.

"Cloak of Darkness" (Season 1, episode 9) Ventress liberates Nute Gunray from Republic imprisonment, and duels Ahsoka Tano and Luminara Unduli to a stalemate in her escape.

Lucas expressed an affinity for strong female characters in several interviews. She mapped that sensibility into Ventress's storyline in *The Clone Wars*, describing the character as an expression of "visceral female rage."

Since around the turn of the century, fan academics have been extolling the influence of *Buffy the Vampire Slayer* on pop culture at conventions and in scholarly writing in books like *Fan Phenomena: Buffy the Vampire Slayer*. With *Buffy* showrunner Joss Whedon now helming superhero blockbusters and writer Jane Espenson branching out to shows like the ABC hit drama *Once Upon a Time*, the relevance of *Buffy the Vampire Slayer* on the direction of popular storytelling may continue to be a topic for many years to come. The long-running arcs of characters like Cordelia, Faith, Drusilla, and Glory created roadmaps for future storytellers to understand that female characters do not have to all be likeable or good in order for an audience to root for them. *Buffy* and *Tank Girl* inspired Katie Lucas to take a villain, one who could have remained a sort of pastiche of the female bad girl, and elevate her to the status of anti-hero-ine, a character who might do bad things, but the audience still hopes she prevails.

"ARC Troopers" (Season 3, episode 2) While General Grievous's droid army invades Kamino to strike at the Republic's critical cloning facilities, Ventress's task is to steal the original Jango Fett genetic sample. She nearly succeeds, but Anakin stops her.

A HERO REVEALED?

Clockwise, from right: At her most brutal; the betrayal of Captain Argyus; ready for redemption? Seeing the future bounty hunter as a child made Ventress a more sympathetic character than she first appeared; a skilled warrior, Ventress is powerful enough to take on more than one Jedi.

Over the course of *The Clone Wars'* run, Ventress crosses paths with a character spawned from the early Sith witch concept art, Nightsister leader Mother Talzin. A complicated history is woven between the two formative women that shapes our understanding of Ventress, who had been born a Nightsister and offered up to a criminal in order to protect the future of the matriarchal clan. In her backstory the classic elements of a hero archetype begin to appear, which might not be surprising given Katie Lucas's mentor was her father, George Lucas.

So who is Asajj Ventress? She is a Nightsister sacrificed to slavery as a child, then saved and trained by a Jedi mentor she eventually loses. Where Luke had a mentor and friends to keep his path firmly entrenched in the light side, Ventress is left alone and gives in to dark side temptations. As Sith do, Count Dooku exploits her abilities for his own gain, and the audience really gets to see glimpses of her true self as she is reborn a Nightsister. Unlike the compact arcs of the movies, *The Clone Wars* gave Asajj Ventress the chance to follow in the footsteps of Luke Skywalker, Anakin Skywalker, and even Buffy Summers; Ventress experiences multiple character journey cycles, peeling back yet more layers over the course of the television series. What we do know is that finding a family in the Nightsisters would be short-lived, and Dooku's retribution would cause Asajj to be left alone, yet again, when her clan is slaughtered by General Grievous's army.

From there, we have clues of Asajj's new path. Embarking on a life as a bounty hunter, her empathy for fugitive Jedi Ahsoka Tano leads

ASAJJ VENTRESS'S PATH THUS FAR LEADS TO A FORK IN THE ROAD.

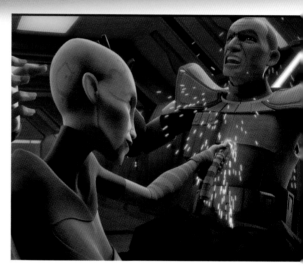

"Nightsisters," "Monster" & "Witches of the Mist" (Season 3, episodes 12-14) Ventress returns to her homeworld of Dathomir, reuniting with the witch leader Mother Talzin. After a failed attempt to assassinate Count Dooku, Talzin's Nightsister magicks transform Savage Opress into a fearsome warrior to mount a second strike at the Sith Lord.

"Massacre" (Season 4, episode 19) Dooku dispatches Grievous to wipe out the Nightsister clan. Despite the witches' best efforts, Talzin and Ventress are the only survivors.

"Bounty" (Season 4, episode 20) Following a new path as a bounty hunter, Ventress joins a crew assembled by Boba Fett to undertake a subterranean transport mission.

to a remarkable turn of events when Ventress allies with the Padawan, even offering critical information to Ventress's longtime adversary, Anakin Skywalker, that helps clear Ahsoka's name. While the creative team on *The Clone Wars* had much more in store for the character, the show came to an end with a fitting heroic-arc style closure for its central character, Ahsoka Tano. At Comic-Con International: San Diego last summer, Dave Filoni revealed that Asajj's story would indeed be continued in the form of the adult novelization *Dark Disciple*, based on eight episodes written by Katie Lucas.

Asajj Ventress's path thus far leads to a fork in the road that has potential to branch in any number of ways. There could be a heroic rise or a tragic fall. Either way, *Star Wars* has done both paths exceptionally well, and it will be fascinating to see where the journey takes her, and the new shades she will cast in our collective understanding of how character arcs can create impactful stories.◉

---MORE TO SAY---

Tricia Barr is co-author on *Ultimate Star Wars* from DK Publishing. Connect with her on Twitter @fangirlcantina.

HAVE YOU?

Brothers" & "Revenge" (Season 4, episodes 21-22)
Maul and Opress wreak havoc in the criminal underworld. After they capture Obi-Wan, Ventress takes up the bounty posted by the Jedi Council and successfully rescues Kenobi from their clutches.

"To Catch a Jedi" & "The Wrong Jedi" (Season 5 episodes 19-20)
When Ahsoka is framed for treason, she flees into the underbelly of Coruscant. Ventress makes an unlikely ally for the fugitive Padawan, but she provides crucial clues that help Anakin clear his apprentice's name.

Dark Disciple (unproduced for television, released as a book)
A stunning new chapter for Asajj Ventress, proving that there is plenty of life in the sultry avenger...

aurra sing: tracked down

THE NEW FACE OF DARTH VADER!

STAR WARS
INSIDER

special 50th Issue
collector's edition

HAYDEN CHRISTENSEN

an exclusive interview with

THE newest anakin

HAYDEN CHRISTENSEN
ANAKIN SKYWALKER

ISSUE 50
JULY/AUGUST 2000

THIS MONTH, FAR, FAR AWAY....

Marvel *Star Wars* artist Chic Stone passes away

The New Jedi Order: Agents of Chaos I: Hero's Trial released

Sir Alec Guinness passes away

Star Wars: Union released

A relative newcomer when he was cast as Anakin Skywalker in *Attack of the Clones*, Hayden Christensen had the difficult job of bridging the gap between Jake Lloyd's pre-teen Ani and the adult Sith Lord who storms aboard the *Tantive IV* in the opening moments of *A New Hope*. Christensen was equal to the task, however, and his strong physical presence, brooding intensity, and onscreen rapport with Ewan McGregor's Obi-Wan Kenobi helped convey the sense of impending tragedy that informed the entire prequel trilogy.— **Jonathan Wilkins**

Hayden Christensen was born on April 19, 1981. An actor and producer, he began his career on Canadian television at the age of 13, then diversified into American television in his late teens. His performance in the movie Life as a House *(2001), earned him Golden Globe and Screen Actors Guild award nominations. He was nominated for the Saturn Award for Best Actor and won the Cannes Film Festival Revelation Award for his portrayal of Anakin Skywalker.*

I was a teenage SITH LORD

INTERVIEW BY **Scott Chernoff**
BLACK AND WHITE PHOTOGRAPHY BY **Samuel Nathan Primero**

INTRODUCING Anakin Skywalker

CANADIAN ACTOR HAYDEN CHRISTENSEN, 19, TALKS TO THE *INSIDER* ABOUT TAKING OVER THE MOST IMPORTANT ROLE IN THE *STAR WARS* SAGA—ANAKIN SKYWALKER, THE JEDI KNIGHT WHO WILL BECOME DARTH VADER.

HAYDEN CHRISTENSEN IS ANAKIN SKYWALKER. HAYDEN CHRISTENSEN IS DARTH VADER. BUT WHO IS HAYDEN CHRISTENSEN?

the question is understandable, since the casting of Anakin Skywalker, perhaps the coolest, most complex archetype in cinema history, was one of the motion picture industry's most-anticipated and speculated-about decisions in recent memory.

Fans wanted to know the answer to one of the *Star Wars* saga's oldest questions: what did Darth Vader look like *before* he put on that famous black helmet? And Hollywood wanted to know which lucky young actor would be chosen to star in two likely blockbusters—would it be Leo? One of the *Dawson's Creek* kids? Or maybe some guy who's never acted but was mentioned on the Internet?

All along, George Lucas insisted the actor he chose would be an unknown, just like Mark Hamill, Harrison Ford, and Carrie Fisher, the stars of his original trilogy, were in 1977. He stayed true to his word, choosing an obscure but charismatic young Canadian actor whose most prominent role to date was as a troubled teen on the Fox Family Channel cable series *Higher Ground*.

Christensen—who will play Anakin in both Episodes II and III—emerged out of over 400 actors from a nationwide, months-long talent search undertaken by Robin Gurland, the casting director who also brought Jake Lloyd (the nine-year-old Anakin in Episode I) to George Lucas' attention. With Episode II taking place roughly 10 years later, one more person was

needed to join the pantheon of actors who have portrayed the character, including Lloyd, David Prowse (who wore the Darth Vader costume in the classic trilogy), James Earl Jones (who supplied Vader's voice), stuntman Bob Anderson (who handled most of Vader's lightsaber battles), and Sebastian Shaw (the late actor who played the older Anakin in *Return of the Jedi*).

A native of Vancouver (his family later moved to Toronto, where he grew up with a brother and two sisters), Christensen is also an athlete who nearly pursued tennis instead of acting. In addition to *Higher Ground*, he had a regular role on the Canadian soap *Family Passions* when he was just 13, appeared in the films *In the Mouth of Madness* and the recent *The Virgin Suicides*, and had roles in a number of television movies, including *Love and Betrayal: The Mia Farrow Story* and the recent *Freefall* and *Lost in a Purple Haze*.

But clearly, Hayden Christensen's biggest role is yet to come. And what a role—he gets to portray Anakin Skywalker during both his rise as a Jedi Knight and his fall to the dark side as a Lord of the Sith. He must convey the goodness of Jake Lloyd's Anakin and the vicious, remorseless evil of Darth Vader, the guy who choked Imperials just for kicks. He gets to swing a lightsaber, summon the Force, and romance Natalie Portman. He is the father of Luke Skywalker, the father of Princess Leia.

That's why the *Insider* thought it was important to get to know Hayden Christensen beyond the list of movies he's done or sports he's played. Like we all wondered when the casting announcement was made in May, who is this guy, anyway?

Just days after he won the role of Anakin Skywalker, the actor sat down with us for his first exclusive *Insider* interview at his agent's office in Beverly Hills. As soon as he walked in the door, it was easy to see why he stood out among all the Anakin hopefuls. Christensen was warm, easy-going, and laughed a lot—but he was also articulate, serious about his craft, and intense in his commitment to it. Answering every question easily, Christensen gave us plenty of time to get to the bottom of who he is.

CONGRATULATIONS, HAYDEN!

Thanks!

AFTER YOU WERE CAST, LUCASFILM WAITED TO ANNOUNCE YOUR NAME UNTIL ALL THE CONTRACTS WERE SIGNED AND PAPERWORK WAS COMPLETED. WHAT WAS THAT WEEK LIKE, WHEN THE ONLY PEOPLE YOU COULD TELL WERE YOUR FAMILY AND FRIENDS?

It was tough. I didn't even tell most of my friends. Just my best friend and some of my family members knew. I wasn't allowed to tell anybody. I was half-convinced that it was this big scheme that they were running, because there was all this anticipation over who was going to get the role. I figured I was sort of like their decoy, that they were going to say that I had it, just to throw everybody off, and I didn't really have it, and later they were going to announce someone else. That would have been so cruel. I was so relieved when I signed the contract.

Mostly, though, I just walked around with a huge grin on my face, and everyone asked,

"USUALLY YOU DON'T SIGN ONTO A FILM BEFORE YOU'VE READ THE SCRIPT. BUT THIS IS DEFINITELY THE ONE EXCEPTION."

"Why are you so happy?" I would just say, "You'll find out sooner or later." It's been very surreal. It's the hardest thing, because I love to share.

IT'S PROBABLY JUST THE BEGINNING OF HOLDING BACK ON SHARING DETAILS ABOUT EPISODE II.

Yeah, and it's hard to not tell people, but that's what we've got to do.

WHERE WAS THAT WEEK SPENT—AT HOME IN VANCOUVER?

Yes, I was doing a television show called *Higher Ground*. We shot there for eight months. We did 20 episodes. I was actually born in Vancouver, and that was my first time back there. So it felt like home, I love it there. I keep my apartment there, but my family lives in Toronto. I love Toronto, too—very low key and friendly vibe.

KIND OF DIFFERENT THAN OUT HERE IN L.A., HUH?

Yeah, I've been out in Los Angeles for about a month now, and I thought I would enjoy it more than I am. Los Angeles, or Hollywood, just seems so full of ambition—overcrowded with ambition. It's overwhelming. I always thought it would be this place where artists could come for a place to create, which it's not really. It's much more commerce here than it is art, which took me by surprise.

HOW RECENTLY DID YOU FIND OUT YOU GOT THE PART—TWO WEEKS AGO?

Less than that, actually—about a week and a half.

HAVE YOU GOTTEN RECOGNIZED ON THE STREET ALREADY?

Yes! It's chaos already. We went to Mr. Chow's for dinner with my agent, and I guess someone tipped them off that we were there. There was a swarm of people when we came out. I'd never really experienced that before—you just get inundated with so many questions. I've never been through that before, so it was weird.

WERE YOU HOPING TO ATTAIN THAT KIND OF FAME?

It was never something I really thought about. As an actor, you don't really think of how well you're doing in terms of your level of fame. It's rather the quality of your work.

DO YOU KNOW ANYTHING ABOUT THE STORY OF EPISODE II YET?

I don't know anything. I'm as much in the dark as everybody else. It's really weird, because usually you don't sign onto a film before you've read the script. But this is definitely the one exception.

WHAT MAKES IT THE ONE EXCEPTION IN YOUR MIND?

Because it's *Star Wars*! It speaks for itself—come on.

HAS IT BEGUN TO SINK IN AT ALL THAT YOU'RE STEPPING INTO THE CENTRAL CHARACTER OF THE BIGGEST MOVIE SERIES OF ALL TIME? CAN IT EVEN SOUND REAL YET?

No, and I don't think it ever will. You know, it still feels very surreal. I'm beside myself. It's like I'm sitting next to myself, seeing myself, and asking, "Are you understanding this?"—"No, are *you* understanding this?" It's incredible. I never would have thought this would happen. I'm nervous, I'm excited, I'm overwhelmed. I'm experiencing so many different emotions right now. It's a lot to deal with. But I'm thrilled with the challenge.

WALK US THROUGH THE AUDITION PROCESS. YOUR FIRST MEETING WAS WITH ROBIN GURLAND, THE CASTING DIRECTOR. DID YOU READ FOR HER AT THAT POINT?

No, the first time was just a general meeting with Robin. I was in Vancouver doing *Higher Ground*, and I flew out just to meet with her, over at some hotel down the street, actually. We just had a normal conversation. We didn't talk about *Star Wars*, just about my experiences with acting and what I was doing. She put that on videotape, and George saw that.

Then, about two months later, I met with George over at Skywalker Ranch. And that was nothing but cool. It was my first time there, and it's very picturesque, and very surreal. You've got llamas grazing fields nearby, and it's beautiful, and then you walk into George's office and

there he is. George Lucas. It was exciting for me. We just sat down and we talked—not about *Star Wars*. We didn't even talk about the film industry, really. It was just normal chit-chat.

SIZING EACH OTHER UP?

Well, more him sizing me up, and me trying to, you know, be sized up well.

AT THAT TIME, THE BIG RUMOR CIRCULATING WAS THAT THE TOP CONTENDER FOR ANAKIN WAS LEONARDO DICAPRIO. DID YOU THINK YOU HAD A CHANCE?

I never really felt like it would come to fruition, that I would ever even test for it. It was just more of a field trip for me, going in and meeting George and getting to see the Ranch. When I found out that I was going to test for it, I still never thought it would happen. It was just cool, and that's it.

HOW MUCH LONGER AFTER YOUR MEETING WITH GEORGE WAS YOUR SCREEN TEST?

I went back about two months later to do the test screen with Natalie, which was great, because I've always respected her work.

HAVE YOU SEEN *THE PROFESSIONAL*?

Oh, yeah—I'm a fan of all her films. I think she's made some really smart choices in the work that she has done. I'm really excited to be working with her, and Ewan too. He's great, so that will be fun.

WAS IT EASY READING WITH NATALIE THE FIRST TIME? WHAT WERE YOU READING?

It was great. It was a scene that's not going to be used in the actual film, but it was still in context to *Star Wars*.

DID THEY GIVE THAT TO YOU IN ADVANCE?

Yes, I got that a couple of weeks before the test, and I made sure that I knew it like the back of my hand. But it was hard, because I didn't have a script to help me get a better idea of who this character was. Even though you know he's Darth Vader and there are all these other films about him, I wasn't sure where he was in the development, in the progression of Anakin to Darth. So, it was hard going into it. I was sort of in the dark.

"IT WAS SO COOL. I WAS CONTENT WITH JUST THE EXPERIENCE (OF THE SCREEN TEST). I GOT TO SHOOT A SCENE FROM *Star Wars*!"

But when I sat down with George, I got a better sense of what I was supposed to be doing. And when you see George, he's kind of like a rock star—he has this entourage that just follows him around. But when you're alone with him and he's giving you direction, he makes you feel very at ease. He's very disarming.

So then Robin, Natalie, George, and I went to a separate room just to rehearse it a few times. We ran over the lines, and then we went into where we were going to shoot the screen test. Then we rehearsed the scene a couple of times on camera, and then we shot it. And we did reverses and close-ups, until George was happy with what we did.

So he shot it like a short film?

Yeah! It was so cool—I was content with just the experience. I got to shoot a scene from *Star Wars*! They gave me an Episode I cap, too, and a nice *Star Wars* mug. I got a few souvenirs, and I was happy.

Beyond practicing the lines, how else did you prepare for the screen test? Did you pull out any of the four other movies?

Oh, yeah, I watched them religiously for a week beforehand. I wanted to make sure I was as prepared as possible. I also remember I picked up a copy of your magazine before I went to go and meet with George. I was like, "They have their own magazine?!" That is so cool.

Amazing but true. What effect did watching the Star Wars films have on your audition?

Well, George has a very specific way of writing in the *Star Wars* context. It's not a normal way of speaking. I wanted to get a feel for that for the most part, familiarize myself more with some of the *Star Wars* themes, and get an idea of the sensibilities that Jake Lloyd and Sebastian Shaw brought to the character—just to get an idea of what they were bringing to Anakin. I picked up on some of those things.

What did you pick up on?

Well, Jake brought this very innocent, very naive side to the character. And Sebastian brought a very pure intensity to the role.

So after the screen test, you went back to Vancouver, and got a phone call, right?

I was in bed, and my roommate walked into my room and handed me the phone. It was my agent and they sounded really excited, so I knew immediately what was going on. I just walked outside for a minute, and then I called my mom.

How are your friends and family reacting to your new role?

They're all very happy for me. I think that I've surrounded myself with very good people, so nothing's really changed for me, it's pretty much the same. But this is just going to be so cool, seeing myself wielding lightsabers and using the Force. Who gets to do that?

I read that you were going to train in the martial arts style of Bo.

I was going to take some Bo classes just for myself, to familiarize myself with some of the moves. But I was just told *not* to do that actually, and to take fencing instead, which will give me a better idea. So, I'm going to take some fencing classes before I get to Australia. I go out the beginning of June, and I work with Nick Gillard, who is the stunt coordinator, for about three weeks, everyday, learning the different fight scenes. I'm going to try to do most of my own stunts.

You're already an athlete, right?

Yes. I come from an athletic family. My father went to university on a football scholarship, and my brother was a runner. He went to the University of Pennsylvania on a running scholarship. And I've played competitive tennis and competitive hockey. My original plan was to go to university on a tennis scholarship, but I got side-tracked with acting.

How did you get side-tracked?

By doing *Higher Ground*. But I've been acting since I was seven.

So acting won out over tennis?

Yes. I've put my academics on hold for right how. I don't know what I'm going to do after we finish filming the next *Star Wars*—go back to school, make another film, both—or go travel. I'm not sure. But this is what I've always wanted to do. This has always been my dream.

So you consider yourself more of an actor than an athlete?

Definitely. But I wanted to go to university and have that experience.

You went to a performing arts high school. Was it like *Fame*?

No, it was actually a performing arts program within a mainstream high school. So to go to the high school, I had to audition and be accepted, but I only took one performing arts

"WHEN EPISODE I CAME OUT, MY ENTIRE HIGH SCHOOL VACATED, JUST TO GO SEE THE FIRST SHOWING OF IT."

course, drama. The rest of my courses were with a mainstream high school, math and everything else. But that's what gave me the acting bug. My teachers there were so inspirational in guiding me through this process. I owe a lot to them.

HOW DID YOU START ACTING AS A CHILD?

I got into the business when I was about seven. My older sister was Junior World Champion on the trampoline, and they wanted her to do a Pringles potato chips commercial. She did it, and then afterward they suggested she get an agent. When she went to go meet with one of these agencies, there was no one home to baby-sit me. I was just along for the ride, and they asked me if I wanted to do a few commercials. I said sure. And that's how I originally got into it. But I didn't get the acting bug until I was in high school.

WHAT IS IT ABOUT ACTING THAT YOU LOVE?

It's the ability to reinvent yourself. There are so many things that I myself would never do, but I have the ability to live vicariously through my characters. They say it's the shy man's revenge—which in my case it definitely is.

YOU THINK YOU'RE PRETTY SHY?

I'd say so. But acting definitely brings it out of me.

YOU DON'T SEEM SHY.

Yeah, interviews are different.

HAD YOU DONE A LOT OF INTERVIEWS BEFORE ALL OF THIS?

No. I started to get introduced to the whole idea during *Higher Ground*, so that prepared me a little bit.

GETTING THE ROLE ON *HIGHER GROUND* MUST HAVE FELT LIKE YOUR BIG BREAK AT THE TIME.

I never really wanted to do television. I always wanted to make films. I've always had a love for film, and the reason why I developed such an interest in acting was because at the time that was the only way I could be involved in films. I couldn't direct, I couldn't produce, I couldn't do any of the other creative stuff like that, and that's why I got into it.

AND NOW YOU'VE MADE A FIVE-YEAR COMMITMENT TO YOUR NEXT TWO FILMS.

And I couldn't be happier—what a film to commit to!

YOU RECENTLY APPEARED IN *THE VIRGIN SUICIDES*, DIRECTED BY SOFIA COPPOLA.

Well, if you look hard, you'll see me in the background running by. I have a few lines, but I'm not one of the leads.

YOU KNOW, SOFIA COPPOLA IS IN EPISODE I AS ONE OF THE QUEEN'S HANDMAIDENS.

No way! Are you kidding me? I had no idea. That's pretty cool.

YOU'VE PLAYED WOODY ALLEN'S SON IN A TV-MOVIE, AND A CREEPY KID ON A BIKE IN JOHN CARPENTER'S *IN THE MOUTH OF MADNESS*. DO YOU HAVE A FAVORITE PRE-STAR WARS ROLE?

All my favorite work so far has been on stage. I've done a couple professional productions. I did *Hamlet*. That would probably be my favorite part—Hamlet.

FROM HAMLET TO VADER.

[Pretending to be weighing two sides of a scale] Hmm, Hamlet, Vader. Hamlet, Vader.

AREN'T YOU A MUSICIAN TOO?

I play the piano and some other instruments.

WHAT KIND OF PIANO DO YOU PLAY?

Jazz, Blues—I can't read a note of it, but I've been playing since I was about seven.

WHAT KIND OF MUSIC DO YOU LISTEN TO?

I listen to everything—OutKast, Ben Harper. I don't really listen to country, but I listen to most everything else.

WHAT DO YOU DO WHEN YOU HANG OUT WITH YOUR FRIENDS?

I don't know. Go shoot stick, just normal stuff. Find something to do. Usually we just sit around contemplating what we want to do.

WHAT DO YOU READ?

I read a lot of magazines. *Colors*, *Details*, there's a slew of them that I have at home. *Star Wars Insider*! *[Laughs.]*

WHAT ARE YOUR FAVORITE MOVIES?

The Princess Bride is probably at the top of the list. *Living in Oblivion*. And *Without Limits*, I like that movie a lot. It's with Billy Crudup – it's the Steve Prefontaine story. They made two of them, and it's the good one.

OTHER THAN *HIGHER GROUND*, WHAT DO YOU WATCH ON TV?

Well, to be honest, I've never seen an episode of *Higher Ground* on TV—I don't have cable. But I love *The Simpsons*.

WHO IS YOUR FAVORITE CANADIAN STAR?

Do we have many? The Canadians are breaking out now—we're taking over. Who was it that I just found out was Canadian? Macy Gray is Canadian, I just got her CD. I'll say Macy Gray.

BRYAN ADAMS—PRO OR CON?

Con. Celine Dion—con. We apologize for them.

DO YOU HAVE A FAVORITE STAR WARS MOVIE? YOU'VE WATCHED THEM QUITE A BIT LATELY.

I'd have to say the first one, because it was so ahead of its time. It was so revolutionary in terms of filmmaking—all of his films are, but I'd say the first one was my favorite.

DO YOU HAVE A FAVORITE STAR WARS CHARACTER?

Vader! *[Laughs]*

ANYONE BESIDES VADER?

Yoda. I love Yoda.

I JUST FIGURED I'D GET IN AS MANY QUESTIONS AS I COULD BEFORE YOU GOT TOO BUSY.

Nah, I've got time. This is *Star Wars*—this is me!

THIS *IS* YOU. ISN'T THAT AWESOME?

It's weird. It's almost too much to deal with.

IS IT WEIRD THINKING THAT *STAR WARS* BEGAN BEFORE YOU WERE EVEN BORN?

Well, *Star Wars* has always been a part of my

"*THE PRINCESS BRIDE* IS PROBABLY AT THE TOP OF THE LIST. *LIVING IN OBLIVION*, AND *WITHOUT LIMITS*, I LIKE THAT MOVIE A LOT."

life, though. I grew up on it, so it seems weird in that sense. *Star Wars* was, of course, before my time, but everyone's seen it and everyone loves it. The fans are just so devoted. We were big into *Star Wars* and all the paraphernalia. My brother had every figure, every starship. He's 27, and he's fanatical about *Star Wars*.

When Shadows of the Empire came out on Nintendo 64, we used to lock ourselves in my bedroom and relay the controller back and forth until we became Jedi Knights. If I played it too much, I remember, it used to visit me in my dreams. I used to have dreams that I was in the *Star Wars* game. It just had such an impact.

WHAT WERE YOUR SHADOWS OF THE EMPIRE DREAMS LIKE?

Everything was very boxy, and very digital-ized. That game was great.

WHAT DID YOU LIKE BEST ABOUT STAR WARS WHEN YOU WERE A KID?

Just the—you know—everything! It was just so different from everything else that I'd seen, and it affected so many other people that I knew. Some of my friends are fanatical about *Star Wars*. When Episode I came out, my entire high school vacated, just to go to the first show-ing of it. We all rushed to the theaters to see the noon showing of *Star Wars*. We also bought tickets for the theatrical trailers—we paid seven bucks, and then we left when the movie started.

WHAT DID YOU THINK OF EPISODE I WHEN YOU FIRST SAW IT?

I thought it was great. I loved it. It was such a cool film. You know, I was always curious what Darth Vader was going to look like under the mask.

AND NOW, YOU KNOW HE LOOKS LIKE YOU.

Yeah—whoa.

OF ALL THE ACTORS WHO HAVE PORTRAYED ANAKIN, YOU'RE GETTING HIM AT PER-HAPS THE MOST INTERESTING POINT OF HIS LIFE.

It's going to be a pretty cool development. You know, aside from the fact that it's *Star Wars*, and it has this cultural following, and it's a huge event, I'm thrilled to be working on it mostly because it has all these mythic qualities and reli-gious parallels. As an actor it's going to be very challenging. I'm looking forward to it.

HOW DOES THIS CHARACTER COMPARE TO OTHERS YOU'VE PLAYED?

It's a complete 180 degrees from what I was doing before. So I'm excited. Plus, I've never worked on a film of this scale. That's exciting, too.

WHAT IS YOUR EXPERIENCE WITH SPECIAL EFFECTS?

Zero to none. Most of the work I've done has been in low budget films. *Higher Ground* didn't have a very big budget.

HAVE YOU EVER PLAYED A BAD GUY BEFORE?

My character on *Higher Ground* was a bad kid. He was a troubled, drug-abusing, messed-up, sexually abused punk. He's not a bad kid though. He's just messed up. He's confused. I don't think anyone at that age is innately bad, there's just some confusion. But if you watch the show, there's definitely a progression, and a development to some understanding of what was happening in his life that was making him make these mistakes.

ACCORDING TO STAR WARS LORE, AT SOME POINT DARTH VADER HUNTS DOWN AND SLAUGHTERS ALL THE JEDI.

Yeah. It's going to be weird making that tran-sition from pretty much the pinnacle of good—which Jake embodies—to the most powerful man in the universe, the darkest, evilest Darth.

WHEN I WATCH THE MOVIES, IT'S HARD TO RECONCILE LITTLE JAKE LLOYD WITH DARTH VADER. IT SEEMS LIKE A WHOLE DIFFERENT PERSON TO ME. ARE YOU NERVOUS ABOUT BRIDGING THAT GAP?

Of course I'm nervous. I think something would be wrong if I wasn't nervous. But I've got two films to make that transition, and George is going to outline it. It will be a challenging task, but it will be a fun collaboration between myself and George.

CLEARLY HE SAW SOMETHING IN YOU THAT GAVE HIM CONFIDENCE. WHAT DO YOU THINK IT IS ABOUT YOU AS AN ACTOR OR A PERSON THAT HELPED HIM SEE THE POTENTIAL FOR BOTH THOSE SIDES?

I don't know—if I were to say anything, it would be boasting.

DO YOU KNOW IF YOU'LL BE PUTTING ON THE HELMET?

I don't know—but I know it would be pretty cool though! It was funny, because the costume designer, Trisha Biggar, called me up yesterday. She described to me what I was going to be wearing. She said, "You're going to be in your basic Jedi outfit, with your belt to hold your lightsaber." It just sounds weird to hear that—*your lightsaber*. It's the coolest thing.

WHAT ARE YOU MOST LOOKING FORWARD TO ABOUT THIS SUMMER?

There are so many aspects that I'm so thrilled to be involved with. I've never been outside of North America, so this will be my first chance to see some of the other parts of the world—and it's going to be pretty cool to do it on the Lucas Tour Bus!

AND I'M SURE IT ALMOST GOES WITHOUT SAYING YOU'RE EXCITED TO HAVE YOUR OWN ACTION FIGURE?

Yeah—it's cool, having little kids playing with little figurines of my character, or the character that I'm going to portray. He's not just my char-acter. It will be really weird, because *Star Wars* is everywhere. You know, you see Jake's face everywhere. I don't know if I'll ever get used to that. I could be drinking myself out of a Pepsi can. So we'll see—I'll just take it as it comes.

HOW MUCH OF YOUR JOB AS AN ACTOR WILL BE EMULATING THE MANNERISMS OF THE PRIOR ANAKINS—JAKE LLOYD, SEBASTIAN SHAW, DAVID PROWSE, AND JAMES EARL JONES?

Well, of course, there has to be some consis-tency. But the movies are at such different times in Anakin's life that I think I'll have room to play and create. I'm going to try to bring some of the sensibility that Jake brought to the role, and some of the feeling that Sebastian brought to it. But for the most part, I'm going to create my own Anakin—so be prepared. ✦

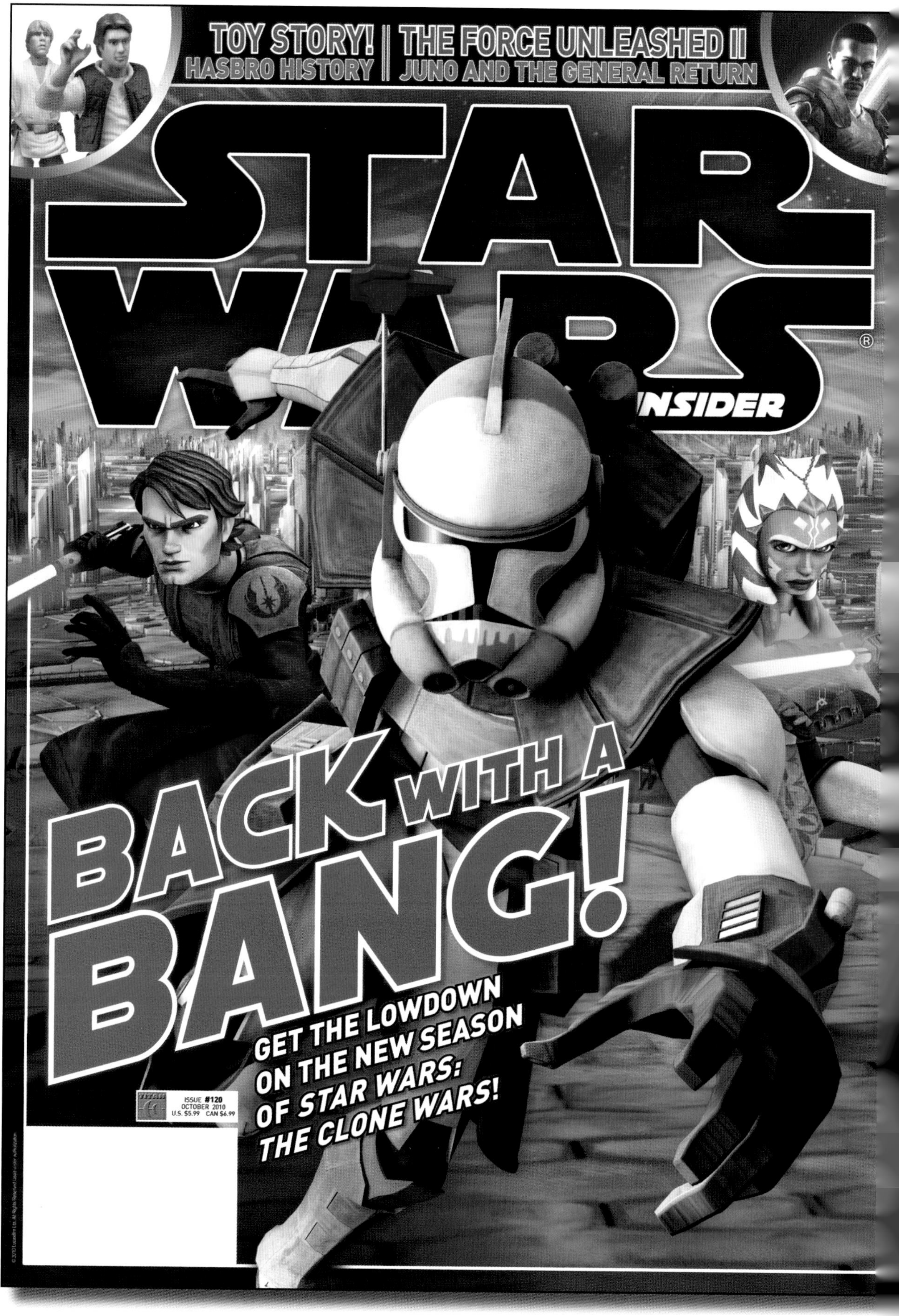

STAR WARS
INSIDER

BACK WITH A BANG!

GET THE LOWDOWN
ON THE NEW SEASON
OF *STAR WARS:*
THE CLONE WARS!

ISSUE **#120**
OCTOBER 2010
U.S. $5.99 CAN $6.99

ANAKIN BETRAYED
REVENGE OF THE SITH

ISSUE 120
OCTOBER 2010

THIS MONTH, FAR, FAR AWAY....

A special edition of *Star Wars Art: Visions* released

The Clone Wars: "Sphere of Influence" aired

The novelization of *The Force Unleashed* II released

The Old Republic 4: Blood of the Empire, Part 1 released

The Clone Wars: "Corruption" aired

The Making of The Empire Strikes Back released

Knight Errant: Aflame 1 released

Few scenes in cinema history have been as long awaited as the showdown between Obi-Wan Kenobi and his errant protégé Anakin Skywalker, in Episode III: *Revenge of the Sith*. Fans have speculated as to what actually happened ever since George Lucas stated in an interview to *Rolling Stone* in 1977 that, "Vader kills Luke's father, then Ben and Vader have a confrontation, just like they have in *Star Wars*, and Ben almost kills Vader... he falls into a volcanic pit and gets fried and is one destroyed being." Back then, readers little suspected that Ben Kenobi was actually fighting his former apprentice; but by 2005 fans fully understood the significance of what they were about to see!—**Jonathan Wilkins**

ANAKIN BETRAYED

WORDS: NEIL EDWARDS

WHAT THEY SAID

"The whole point of [being a] Jedi is you can completely control your anger, and he's at a point where he can't control it at all. It's because of his need for control and power, and being very upset when he doesn't have it. But Obi-Wan is inevitably going to try and stop him. And now he's assuming that she's in league with Obi-Wan, not necessarily in a love relationship or anything, but on the basis that they're on one side, going down one path, and he's going down the other."

George Lucas, *Revenge of the Sith* DVD audio commentary 2005

EXT. MUSTAFAR—LANDING PLATFORM—DAY

The sleek NABOO SKIFF lands on the Mustafar landing platform near Anakin's GREEN STARFIGHTER. ANAKIN runs up to the SKIFF as the ramp lowers. PADMÉ runs to him.

ANAKIN: Padmé, I saw your ship...

They embrace.

PADMÉ: Oh, Anakin!

ANAKIN: It's all right, you're safe now. What are you doing out here?

PADMÉ: I was so worried about you. Obi-Wan told me terrible things.

ANAKIN: What things?

PADMÉ: He said that you have turned to the dark side... that you killed younglings.

ANAKIN: Obi-Wan is trying to turn you against me.

PADMÉ: He cares about us.

ANAKIN: Us??!

PADMÉ: He knows... He wants to help you.

ANAKIN: Is Obi-Wan going to protect you? He can't... he can't help you. He's not strong enough.

WHY IT'S A CLASSIC

This powerful scene illustrates the fact that sometimes in striving to avoid a particular fate, we actually hasten ourselves toward it. That's certainly true in Anakin's case. Anakin has headed toward the dark side and become Palpatine's Sith apprentice to save Padmé from dying—the thing he fears the most. Ironically, it is he who causes her eventual death of a broken heart. Anakin talks of gaining "new powers" so he can save his wife, but he uses this new power by choking Padmé using the dark side of the Force—an act that, thanks to the Emperor's lies, Anakin later believes has killed her. The scene also marks the moment Anakin and Obi-Wan are finally divided. Anakin gives in to his anger and the dark side, while Obi-Wan, seeing the depths his power-mad friend has sunk to, realizes what he must do.

TRIVIA

When the script was still being worked on, one idea that was mooted was that Padmé would decide Anakin had to be killed, and concealed a dagger to attack him with. Some conceptual art was even done depicting Padmé in different costumes and armed with a concealed dagger.

SCRIPT (2003)

PADMÉ: Anakin, all I want is your love.

ANAKIN: Love won't save you, Padmé. Only my new powers can do that.

PADMÉ: At what cost? You are a good person. Don't do this.

ANAKIN: I won't lose you the way I lost my mother! I've become more powerful than any Jedi has ever dreamed of and I've done it for you. To protect you.

PADMÉ: Come away with me. Help me raise our child. Leave everything else behind while we still can.

ANAKIN: Don't you see, we don't have to run away anymore. I have brought peace to the Republic. I am more powerful than the Chancellor. I can overthrow him, and together you and I can rule the galaxy. Make things the way we want them to be.

PADMÉ: I don't believe what I'm hearing... Obi-Wan was right. You've changed.

ANAKIN: I don't want to hear any more about Obi-Wan. The Jedi turned against me. Don't you turn against me.

PADMÉ: I don't know you anymore. Anakin, you're breaking my heart. I'll never stop loving you, but you are going down a path I can't follow.

ANAKIN: Because of Obi-Wan?

PADMÉ: Because of what you've done... what you plan to do. Stop, stop now. Come back! I love you.

ANAKIN: (seeing Obi-Wan) Liar!

PADMÉ turns around and sees OBI-WAN standing in the doorway of the Naboo Cruiser.

PADMÉ: No!

ANAKIN: You're with him. You've betrayed me! You brought him here to kill me!

PADMÉ: No! Anakin, I swear... I...

ANAKIN reaches out, and PADMÉ grabs her throat as she starts to choke.

OBI-WAN: Let her go, Anakin.

ANAKIN: What have you and she been up to?

OBI-WAN: Let her go!

ANAKIN releases his grip on the unconscious PADMÉ and she crumples to the ground.

ANAKIN: You turned her against me.

OBI-WAN: You have done that yourself.

ANAKIN: You will not take her from me.

ANAKIN throws off his cloak.

OBI-WAN: Your anger and your lust for power have already done that.

OBI-WAN flings off his cloak.

OBI-WAN: (continuing) You have allowed this Dark Lord to twist your mind until now... until now you have become the very thing you swore to destroy.

They circle each other until OBI-WAN is near PADMÉ. He places his hand on her.

ANAKIN: Don't lecture me, Obi-Wan. I see through the lies of the Jedi. I do not fear the dark side as you do. I have brought peace, justice, freedom, and security to my new Empire.

OBI-WAN: Your new Empire?

ANAKIN: Don't make me kill you.

OBI-WAN: Anakin, my allegiance is to the Republic... to democracy.

ANAKIN: If you're not with me, you're my enemy.

OBI-WAN: Only a Sith Lord deals in absolutes. I will do what I must. (ignites his lightsaber).

ANAKIN: You will try.

ANAKIN ignites his lightsaber.

EXCLUSIVE LIMITED EDITION COLLECTOR'S COVER

STAR WARS

INSIDER

DARTH VADER

LORD OF THE SITH

ISSUE #108
COLLECTOR'S COVER
April 2009 $5.99

DAVID PROWSE
DARTH VADER

ISSUE 108
APRIL 2009

An imposing figure right from the start of *A New Hope*, Darth Vader owes his powerful physique to champion bodybuilder David Prowse. Diagnosed with tuberculosis at the age of 13, Prowse spent almost a year undergoing treatment in hospital, and then another two years wearing a leg brace. He later reflected that the discomfort of this orthotic prepared him well for donning Vader's suit and mask.

As soon as he was free from his brace, Prowse began swimming to regain strength in his leg. It was on his walk home from a local pool that he decided to become a weightlifter, after seeing the rippling torsos of men on the covers of muscle magazines in a shop window. Beginning at that moment, bodybuilding became Prowse's passion as he was determined to achieve a similar physique.—**Jonathan Wilkins**

David Prowse, MBE, was born on July 1, 1935, and grew up in Bristol in the U.K. He won the British heavyweight weightlifting championship three years running in the 1960s, and played a range of strongman roles on TV and in films during the 1970s. He played the towering figure of Darth Vader in the original trilogy of Star Wars *movies, but did not supply the voice. He is also well known in the U.K. as the face of a long-running road safety campaign.*

DEALING WITH DARTH

WORDS: JONATHAN WILKINS

DAVID PROWSE'S PHYSICAL PERFORMANCE AS THE SINISTER DARTH VADER FIRST CAPTURED AUDIENCES' IMAGINATIONS BACK IN 1977 WHEN HE STRODE ABOARD THE TANTIVE IV. HE HASN'T LOOKED BACK SINCE!

Star Wars Insider: **How did you get the role of such an iconic screen villain?**
David Prowse: I met George Lucas at the 20th Century Fox offices in Soho Square, London. He had seen me in *A Clockwork Orange*, in which I had appeared some years before. He said, "I'm doing this film called *Star Wars*, which is a big space adventure, and I'd like to offer you one of two parts. The first one's a character called Chewbacca. He's like a hairy gorilla who goes through the movie on the side of the goodies." I said, "No, you can keep that one, George, what's the other one?" He said, "The other one's the big villain of the film, a character called Darth Vader." I said, "Don't say any more George, I'll play the villain, thank you!"

Are you still happy to have chosen the bad guy?
I think so. Peter Mayhew did a fantastic job with Chewbacca. I certainly don't think I could have played Chewbacca as well as Peter did.

Can you recall the first time you saw the Vader costume? What was it like to wear?
When I went to see George Lucas for the very first time. He took me into this long room with all these conceptual drawings of the characters and some of the scenes. He showed me an early sketch of Vader and it looked almost like a human fly. It was very weird looking.

Later I met with the costume designer, John Mollo, and got measured for the suit. I didn't see the finished costume until I arrived on set. When they put the helmet and mask on, George asked me to turn my head from left to right. I did but the mask stayed facing forward! They took it off and intended to reduce its size. George said, "No, the mask and helmet fit perfectly

with your shape and size; we'll pad the mask out with foam rubber." And this is what they did. It was really tight.

The suit was comprised of around 15 different pieces. It was all made from quilted leather and fiberglass and had two capes. We filmed during the very hot summer of 1976, so I used to sweat a great deal inside. The heat used to rise up and go into the mask, misting up the eyepieces so I couldn't see! It was OK for about two minutes, but then I had to stop and wipe the eyepieces because I couldn't see where I was going!

Did you have any mishaps as a result?
I didn't walk into the set, but I did knock Alec Guinness over by accident. We were shooting the fight scene in which Vader kills Obi-Wan Kenobi. We were taught the fight by the stunt arranger, Peter Diamond. He used to coach me in a sports arena in North London. When the film started, we'd practice with our sticks between shots. All the practicing we did was in our everyday clothes, or I'd practice with the suit, but without the cape and the helmet. When we filmed the actual fight scene we went through the motions and that was OK. As soon as I started doing something strenuous I sweated, which misted up the eyepieces.

I was supposed to push him away and he would go a couple of paces back and knock into the corridor wall. As soon as I put the mask and helmet on, I couldn't see what I was doing. Unfortunately, I pushed him down the corridor, and he fell over. He dusted himself off and carried on—a true professional.

How long did it take to put the suit on?
I had a dresser we used to call "Mother," and he was ever so helpful in getting me

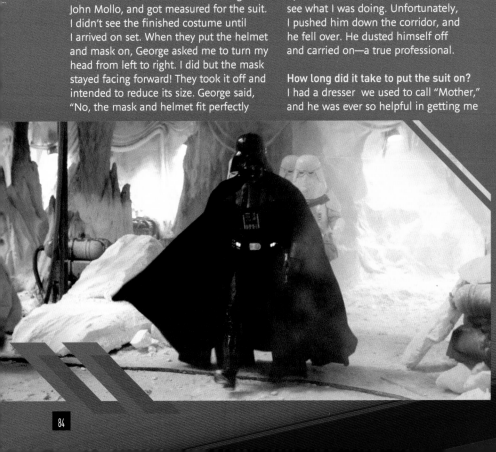

prepared for shooting. We had a dressing room near the set and it would take about 20 minutes to get into the suit. I used to get makeup put on around my eyes because otherwise you could see my eyes flickering behind the mask. They started with opaque lenses, then they used yellow lenses, and eventually dark amber.

I could hardly see where I was going. I also had black makeup around my mouth because my lips could be seen through the mask. I used to look like a big panda!

Was the costume heavy?
It weighed about 40 pounds, but I only wore it for short periods. The mask and helmet were the heaviest. I could sit around all day in the suit with no problem.

When you put the suit on, did people's attitudes change towards you?
No, I don't think so. Everybody was very impressed because, with the helmet and the mask on, I was about seven feet tall! One of the things I did at the beginning was establish the walk, and then everything else fell into place. I decided how I wanted to make everybody subservient apart from Grand Moff Tarkin, who was Vader's boss. So it got to the point where I adopted a brisk, purposeful stride, meaning virtually everybody had to trot quickly alongside me to catch up!

How quickly after the first film was released did you realize that Vader was such an icon?
I did a movie for Russ Meyer called *Black Snake*, and we became friends. Within three days of *Star Wars* coming out, I received

a cable from him. It said, "Congratulations, Dave! You're in the biggest movie of all time. By the way did you know they've over-dubbed your voice?" That was the first time I knew that I was part of an incredible worldwide phenomenon.

What was George Lucas like to work with?
If you give George Lucas what he's looking for then he doesn't interfere. On the very first shot we did, I was walking up a corridor. I was trying to establish Darth Vader's walk and they had a camera track going all the way up the corridor. I strode up the corridor and got to the end. George came over and said, "Sorry David, you've got to slow down. We can't keep up with you!" That was one of the few things he ever said to me about the role and what I was doing.

In *The Empire Strikes Back* we see Vader unmasked from the back, was that you?
Yes, it was me. I was wearing a specially fitted bald-cap that Stuart Freeborn's team made for me.

Is it true that you didn't know about the big revelation at the climax of *The Empire Strikes Back*?
I didn't know I was Luke's father until I went to the premiere. I thought, "Blimey! That's news!" When we were filming on the gantry scene there was a huge airplane propeller creating all the wind. It was making so much noise that I couldn't hear a word that Mark Hamill was saying. All my dialogue was with gestures, so as soon as he had seen me stop gesturing then he would speak and I could see his lips moving.

As soon as he stopped I would come back in with my next line, and that's how we did the scene. I had no idea whatsoever what was actually being said!

Did you enjoy working with Mark?
I did. Mark is a really nice guy. We see each other on the circuit occasionally. He came over for Celebration Europe, and the press made a big thing out of it: father and son reunited [see photo, far right]!

Do you have fun attending fan conventions?
I think they're absolutely phenomenal. I sit down, and my queue for autographs is five hours long and the lines go all around the auditorium and out into the street. And you think, people are lining up for five hours just to get my signature, which amazes me.

LUNCH WITH A JEDI!

David Prowse: "When I got the part of Darth Vader, I was invited to have lunch with Alec Guinness, George Lucas, and Gary Kurtz. We had this lunch and it was obviously to introduce the two of us because I was going to kill him off in the movie. We went into the studio and had a chat with the stunt arrangers. When I saw that Alec Guinness had published his memoirs, I had a look to see if I got an honorable mention. There was one line that said, 'Had lunch today with David Prowse, the actor who is going to play Darth Vader—I fear he is not an actor!'"

When was the last time you wore the Darth Vader costume?
It was around 1997. I appeared in *Rebel Assault II*. They sent the suit to England with a security guard! I noticed my name tag was still in the suit. They sent James Earl Jones' vocal performance over as well so I had to learn all the dialogue and act according to the pre-recorded dialogue, which was quite strange because I'd never done that before.

Have you ever met James Earl Jones?
Never. Someone ought to make a good TV interview of the two of us meeting—the voice meets the body. I'd love to meet him.

Do you have a particular favorite piece of Vader merchandise?
I've just recently gotten a helmet, mask, and breast plate, [supposedly] from an original mold. It's a beautiful piece. And I think Gentle Giant produces some really nice sculptures of Vader.

Do you have a message for Vader fans?
They've been absolutely fantastic! When you consider that something I did all those years ago has obviously captured the imaginations of all these different people. I just feel very privileged to have been the actor that portrayed Darth Vader and thank all the fans for their unwavering support and kindness over the years. ☬

TROOP TALK!
VOICING THE CLONES

MANDALORIANS!
THE ART OF THE ADVENTURE

STAR WARS

INSIDER

ARMED AND DANGEROUS

MATTHEW WOOD
ON SOUNDING OUT
GENERAL GRIEVOUS

CREATING VADER

MEET THE MAN WHO SCULPTED A SITH LORD

PLUS! CAD BANE • VADER VS. SKYWALKER
CHEWBACCA • ROMBA THE EWOK!

ISSUE #116 April 2010
U.S. $7.99 CAN $9.99

BRIAN MUIR
VADER SCULPTOR

ISSUE 116
APRIL 2010

Among the many reasons that account for how *Star Wars* has endured the test of time and technology is surely the high quality of its production. George Lucas made sure that the very best people were employed to realize his exacting vision. One of those people was Brian Muir, whose talents as a sculptor are beyond compare. His prolific output spans numerous James Bond films, *Alien* (1979), *Raiders of the Lost Ark* (1981), *Sleepy Hollow* (1999), *Harry Potter and the Order of the Phoenix* (2007), *Guardians of the Galaxy* (2014), and *Rogue One: A Star Wars Story* (2016). However, it's his work on *Star Wars* in 1977 that assures his immortality.—**Jonathan Wilkins**

Brian Muir was born on April 15, 1952. The sculptor not only created the body armor for the first stormtroopers, the headpieces for several droids, and some finishing work on the C-3PO costume, he also sculpted Darth Vader's helmet and armor, based on concept art by Ralph McQuarrie. Who else can claim their fingers have tweaked Darth Vader's nose?

Star Wars Insider: How did you get started in the movie business? Was it something you always wanted to be involved in?

Brian Muir: I was offered an apprenticeship as a sculptor/ modeler at Elstree Studios in England. There had been 12 unsuccessful candidates for the position before me, but it turned out that I was lucky number 13. Having lived in Borehamwood [England] since I was two years old, I was very aware of all the film studios that were based there, Elstree being one. During my childhood, I had several friends whose family members worked in the studios and it sounded so exciting. But it seemed like a pipe dream to imagine that it would ever be part of my life.

How did you come to work on *Star Wars* and how was the project described to you?'

Arthur Healey, my mentor during my apprenticeship, contacted me to ask if I was available to start work on a new science fiction film at Elstree. All he knew was that it involved sculpting some futuristic characters from different planets and would probably be about six weeks work, but as it turned out I worked on the film for over four months!

BRIAN MUIR
IN THE SHADOW OF VADER

SCULP THE

BRIAN MUIR WAS ASSIGNED THE TASK OF SCULPTING THE ORIGINAL DARTH VADER ARMOR FOR *STAR WARS* AT THE AGE OF 23. LITTLE DID HE KNOW HE WAS HELPING TO CREATE AN ICON! WORDS: JONATHAN WILKINS

Can you talk about the process involved in creating Darth Vader from Ralph McQuarrie's original design?

The process started with Dave Prowse being molded from head to toe so that a full plaster cast could be produced for me to work on. As the mask and helmet were to be sculpted first, the head and shoulders were cut from the body and fixed onto a modeling stand. I began by sculpting the mask, back and front, ensuring that there was at least a quarter inch of clay on the plaster head at any point to allow for casting thickness, and to be sure it would fit well on Dave's head. After creating Vader's mask in clay, it was passed to the plasterers to mold and reproduce in plaster. I then carved and sharpened the plaster cast to a finish. At this point I started modeling the helmet in clay over the plaster mask to ensure the overall appearance worked. The same methods of molding and casting in plaster were again carried out. The final molds were made from the plaster cast, and fiberglass versions were produced.

The plaster head and shoulders were then reaffixed to the body and it was moved to the main plaster shop for me to model the armor. Working from Ralph McQuarrie's paintings, I sculpted the

chest armor, two shoulder bells, and shins. Again each piece was molded and cast in plaster, the lines carved and sharpened with a final remold, and finally cast in fiberglass.

Did this require you to work closely with John Mollo [costume designer], John Barry [production designer], and George Lucas?

I was asked to go to the wardrobe department to see

John Mollo. He gave me a simple line drawing without shading, at a three-quarter angle, of Vader's mask and helmet.

John Barry was the person who I worked closely with during the sculpting process. He came into my workshop each day to see the progress. It was John who suggeste the "tear ducts" and the extension of the tubes past the mouth. In rece years, looking at the McQuarrie paintings, I've noticed the tear ducts were part of the design although the did not appear on John Mollo's sket

Although George Lucas came in the workshop a few times, he made little comment. Once John was happy that the creat of the mask and helmet were complete, he asked George to come into the workshop to give his approval. He seeme very pleased with the result and made no chang

Did you work closely with Davi Prowse?

I didn't work with Dave—in fact I ha no contact with hi I did see him on set on a occasions, but the only ti I've spoken to him was i 2006 when we were bot signing at a memorabilia convention.

Is the approach different for a character who has a lot of screen-time (like Vader) compared to a character who is seen very briefly (like the Death Star droid)?
No, the approach is the same with every piece you're assigned. You do the best you can with whatever you're doing. It's the time constraints imposed by the filming schedules that dictate how much time you can spend on each sculpt, which sometimes reflects in the quality you are able to achieve.

How much creative input did you have on the finished sculpt?
With any sculpt taken from a two-dimensional drawing there is always some creative input from the sculptor. Every sculptor has his or her own personal style and own interpretations of a design.

How long did it take to sculpt the full Vader costume?
I probably spent five weeks total on

Vader. During that time, I was also working on other characters. As the plasterers molded and cast different parts in plaster, I would sharpen them up for remolding and producing the final pieces in fiberglass.

How many Vader helmets were made for the first movie?
There were two finished helmets that were used for the production. They were kept in a locked box that was wheeled onto the stage by the wardrobe department each day. There was also a third helmet produced for the special effects department.

Did you also work on the C-3PO costume?
I did do some work on C-3PO. When

THE OTHER VADER!
By John Brosio and Pete Vilmur

If you're one of the lucky fans to snag a rare pre-release copy of *The Complete Vader* book, you may have been intrigued by the Darth Vader costume depicted on page 17—a costume that appears to have been based on early Ralph McQuarrie concept drawings for the character.

Often mistaken as an early prototype mock-up for the Dark Lord's helmet and chest armor, this was a Halloween costume fabricated by *Star Wars* concept designer Joe Johnston for a Industrial Light & Magic Halloween party in 1976!

Artist and former ILM Creature Shop employee John Brosio, who also happened to create a pretty stunning Vader of his own, recently asked Johnston about the fabled "McQuarrie Vader" costume, and its ultimate fate.

John Brosio: Did you construct the entire costume?
Joe Johnston: Yes, I made it in the model shop after hours. I put in one all-nighter as it got close to Halloween.

Was it styrene? Fiberglass?
It was slump-molded styrene over a fiberglass body mold that had been sent over with one of the costume shipments and discarded. The styrene completely covered the body mold which was a light brown and very rough textured. The helmet was based on a plastic German army helmet from the toy store, with styrene panels and model kit parts attached.

When was it made?
It was made for Halloween in 1976. It was based on Ralph McQuarrie's early illustration of Luke and Vader having their laser sword fight, which is why it doesn't look like the final version of Vader. The color is a blue gray, matching the illustration.

What became of it?
It was stored in a box of *Star Wars* things and was partially crushed when a box of heavier items fell on it as I was preparing to move to Marin County in April of 1978. It was too much trouble to repair so the entire thing went into the trash, except for the helmet.

Could you see out of it?
Yes, very clearly. I used a pair of tinted safety goggles as part of the faceplate.

Is it true that the costume never made it to Northern California?
True, except for the helmet. I saved the helmet for a few years, but pieces started to come off and since it really wasn't the Vader that the world knew, I didn't feel compelled to keep it from its destiny with the dumpster.

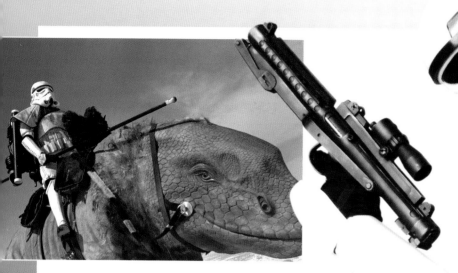

When I started on *Star Wars*, sculptor Liz Moore was just finishing C-3PO at the clay stage. She left the film to join her boyfriend in Holland at the end of January, 1976. It was then left to me to sharpen the detail in the plaster and add the slots across the side joints of the helmet. It was at a very late stage before filming that I was asked to sculpt the hand plates. There was no time to get a plaster cast of Anthony Daniels' hands so I had the unusual job of sculpting directly onto the back of his hands during the lunch break.

Can you tell us about your work on the stormtrooper costumes? Were they sculpted to fit a specific person?
The stormtrooper armor was the first thing I sculpted when I started on the film. I was given a plaster cast of an average-sized person. I began with the chest piece and applied the clay to the plaster cast. As I finished each piece it was molded and cast by the plasterers and, as with Vader, I sharpened the detail at the plaster stage. There were gaps between each piece to allow for movement so the stormtroopers didn't look robotic. Each piece mirrored the

next so that it gave the appearance of a suit of armor but with gaps. The gaps allowed the armor to fit actors of varying sizes—the bigger the actor the bigger the gaps in the armor.

How much consideration is given to the actors? Is there ever trade-off between comfort and design?
Actors are given a certain amount of consideration, but the aesthetics of the costume are very important as well.

Originally there was a back and front to Vader's mask, which was sculpted and produced in fiberglass, but we realized that it would be claustrophobic for Dave, and the back was discarded. Also, to get some more airflow into the mask it was decided at a late stage to add a chin vent. I just drew this in the clay as a guide for the plasterers to cut in the finished fiberglass. Foam was inserted into the mask for a more comfortable fit. Unfortunately, the use of fiberglass does not lend itself to comfort.

Do you prefer creating costumes or set details, such as the space jockey from *Alien*?
I wouldn't say that I have any particular preference. The fine detail of whatever you are working on is satisfying. There is such variety in film work and it is usually interesting, although sometimes challenging. With sculpting the main characters for *Star Wars* there was

a feeling of real involvement in the film rather than working on components of the sets, but from a pure sculpting aspect they are both enjoyable.

If you had the chance to work on Vader again, would you do anything different?
I wouldn't set out to do anything differently, but it would be difficult, even with a trained eye, to produce something that is exactly the same. The fact that Vader has become such an iconic character proves that it worked visually. ☺

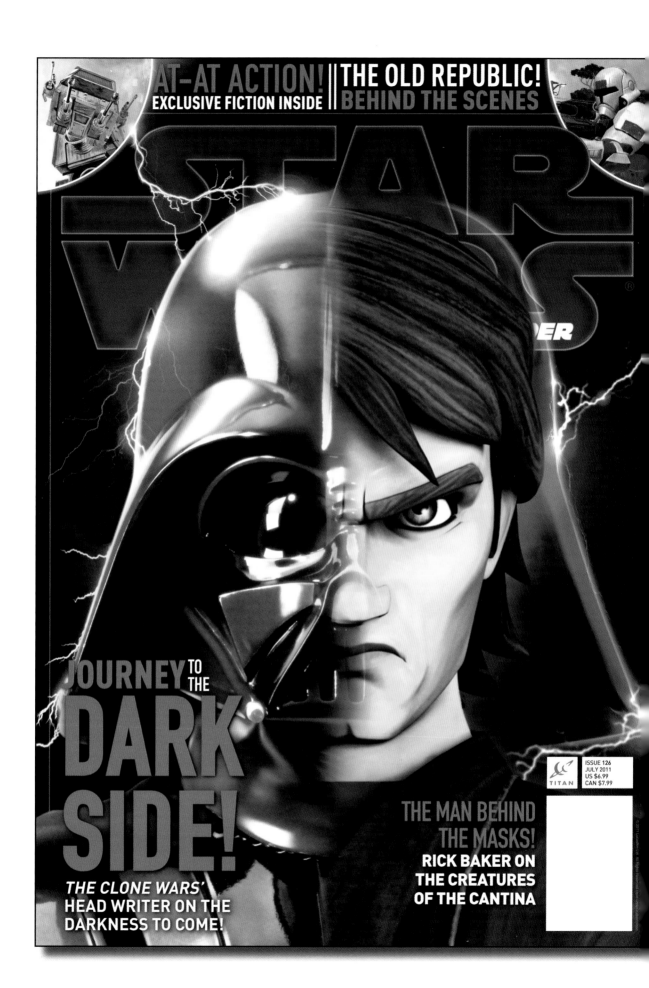

AT-AT ACTION!
EXCLUSIVE FICTION INSIDE

THE OLD REPUBLIC!
BEHIND THE SCENES

STAR WARS

ISSUE 126
JULY 2011
US $6.99
CAN $7.99

TITAN

JOURNEY TO THE
DARK SIDE!

THE CLONE WARS'
HEAD WRITER ON THE
DARKNESS TO COME!

THE MAN BEHIND
THE MASKS!
**RICK BAKER ON
THE CREATURES
OF THE CANTINA**

VADER VS. OBI-WAN
THE CIRCLE IS NOW COMPLETE

ISSUE 126
JULY 2011

THIS MONTH, FAR, FAR AWAY....

Invasion: Revelations 1 released

Star Wars: Knight Errant: Aflame trade paperback released

Choices of One released

Lost Tribe of the Sith: Pantheon released

Jedi—The Dark Side 3 released

The Old Republic—The Lost Suns 2 released

LEGO Star Wars: The Padawan Menace aired on Cartoon Network

The Clone Wars: The Starcrusher Trap released

When audiences first saw *Star Wars* back in 1977, the battle between Obi-Wan Kenobi and Darth Vader had a mythic quality despite—or perhaps because of—the relatively scant screen time afforded to both characters. Given what we now know about these characters via the sequels, prequels, and *The Clone Wars* TV series, the fight takes on whole new levels of meaning as the last time two old adversaries—and two even older friends—meet in the material world.**—Jonathan Wilkins**

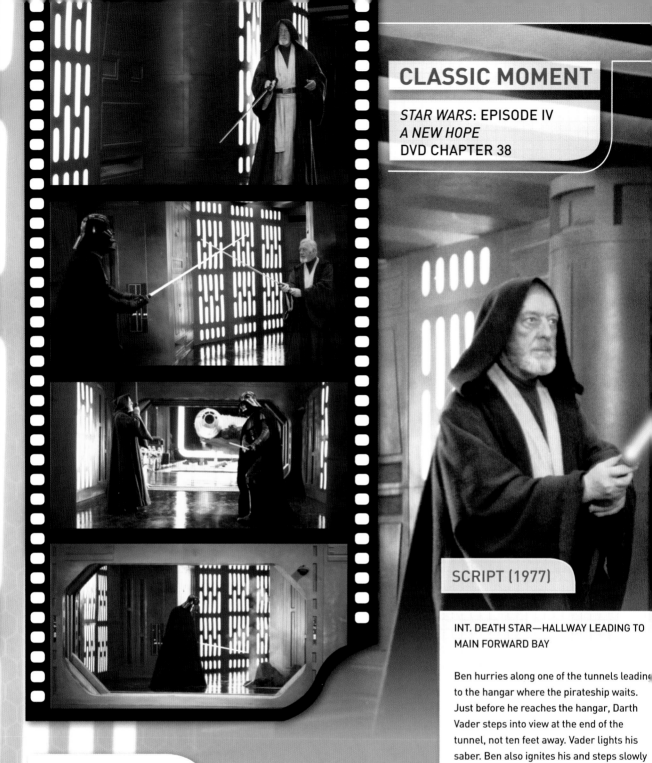

SCRIPT (1977)

INT. DEATH STAR—HALLWAY LEADING TO MAIN FORWARD BAY

Ben hurries along one of the tunnels leading to the hangar where the pirateship waits. Just before he reaches the hangar, Darth Vader steps into view at the end of the tunnel, not ten feet away. Vader lights his saber. Ben also ignites his and steps slowly forward.

VADER: I've been waiting for you, Obi-Wan. We meet again, at last. The circle is now complete.

Ben Kenobi moves with elegant ease into a classical offensive position. The fearsome Dark Knight takes a defensive stance.

VADER: When I left you, I was but the learner; now I am the master.

WHY IT'S A CLASSIC

The first Jedi duel we ever saw in the *Star Wars* saga, Obi-Wan and Vader's confrontation here may lack the acrobatics of many of those to come afterward, but it is one of the most pivotal. As they meet for the first time since their battle on Mustafar—when Vader became half-man, half-machine—there is an inevitability about this climactic encounter. While Vader has been consumed by the dark side, Obi-Wan has been preparing to become one with the Force, which will make him even more powerful. One is the father Luke never knew, while the other is the father figure who has only just come into his life; Luke will never be the same again after he loses Ben. Watching this confrontation, we feel that one generation of Jedi is coming to an end, while the next—the new hope that is Luke—is just beginning.

"YOUR POWERS ARE WEAK, OLD MAN."

BEN: Only a master of evil, Darth.

The two Galactic warriors stand perfectly still for a few moments, sizing each other up and waiting for the right moment. Ben seems to be under increasing pressure and strain, as if an invisible weight were being placed upon him. He shakes his head and, blinking, tries to clear his eyes.

Ben make a sudden lunge at the huge warrior but is checked by a lightning movement of The Sith. A masterful slash stroke by Vader is blocked by the old Jedi. Another of the Jedi's blows is blocked, then countered. Ben moves around the Dark Lord and starts backing into the massive starship hangar. The two powerful warriors stand motionless for a few moments with laser swords locked in mid-air, creating a low buzzing sound.

VADER: Your powers are weak, old man.

BEN: You can't win, Darth. If you strike me down, I shall become more powerful than you can possibly imagine.

Their lightsabers continue to meet in combat.

IN. DEATH STAR—HALLWAY

Solo, Chewie, Luke, and Leia tensely watch the duel. The troops rush toward the battling knights.

HAN: Now's our chance! Go!

They start for the *Millennium Falcon*.

Ben sees the troops charging toward him and realizes that he is trapped. Vader takes advantage of Ben's momentary distraction and brings his mighty lightsaber down on the old man. Ben manages to deflect the blow and swiftly turns around.

The old Jedi Knight looks over his shoulder at Luke, lifts his sword from Vader's, then watches his opponent with a serene look on his face.

Vader brings his sword down, cutting old Ben in half. Ben's cloak falls to the floor in two parts, but Ben is not in it. Vader is puzzled at Ben's disappearance and pokes at the empty cloak. As the guards are distracted, the adventurers and droids reach the starship. Luke sees Ben cut in two and starts for him. Aghast, he yells out.

LUKE: No!

THE OFFICIAL MAGAZINE OF THE *STAR WARS* GALAXY

STAR WARS

INSIDER™

STAR WARS REBELS RETURNS

DAVE FILONI TALKS SEASON THREE

TAYLOR GRAY ON EZRA'S DARK SIDE

TIYA SIRCAR ON WHY THIS IS SABINE'S SEASON

PLUS! SEASON TWO EPISODE GUIDE

ISSUE #169
US $7.99
CAN $9.99
NOV/DEC 2016

THE RISE AND RISE OF DARTH VADER

HOW THE DARK LORD'S SERIES BECAME THE MOST POWERFUL COMIC IN THE GALAXY!

DARTH VADER
MARVEL COMICS

ISSUE 169
NOVEMBER/DECEMBER 2016

The first comic book to be named in honor of a Sith Lord, *Darth Vader* tells the story of the iconic character as he sets out to rebuild his power base following the destruction of the first Death Star. Created by a stellar team—writer Keiron Gillen, artist Salvador Larocca, and editor Jordan D. White and assistant editor Heather Antos at Marvel, and senior editors Jennifer Heddle and Frank Parisi at Lucasfilm—the series became an instant classic, taking its place alongside the very best that four decades of *Star Wars* comics have to offer. Though populated with rich supporting characters that deserve books of their own (paging Doctor Aphra!), the series never forgets that Vader is its star, showing him at his conniving, merciless worst!—**Jonathan Wilkins**

THIS MONTH, FAR, FAR AWAY....

Star Wars: Poe Dameron: Flight Log released

Trapped in the Death Star! released

Star Wars: Aliens and *Ships of the Galaxy* released

Luke and the Lost Jedi Temple released

Star Wars: Galactic Atlas released

"Imperial Super Commandos" premiered on Disney XD

Poe Dameron 8: The Gathering Storm, Part I released

Star Wars: The Force Awakens miniseries concludes with the publication of *The Force Awakens*, Part VI.

Catalyst published.

Star Wars: Heroes For a New Hope released

Star Wars: The Force Awakens 3D Collector's Edition Blu-ray released

SITH STAR

FOR MANY, DARTH VADER IS THE DEFINING ICON OF THE STAR WARS SAGA. YET FOR ALL HIS PRESENCE IN THE ORIGINAL TRILOGY —AND HIS FORESHADOWING IN THE PREQUELS— IT TOOK A GROUNDBREAKING COMIC SERIES TO REALLY MAKE THE SITH THE STAR! WORDS: MICHAEL KOGGE

Star Wars Insider: Darth Vader helped kickstart Marvel's Star Wars comics line in 2015. How did it come to be one of the two launch titles?

Jordan D. White: One of the first ideas we had for the line was that we would have multiple ongoing series that happened simultaneously. It was definitely a departure from what had been done with Star Wars comics before, but it was much more in line with what Marvel does. When you buy comics for the various Avengers titles, they all take place together; and while they can be read separately, reading them together creates a richer universe. We wanted to do that with Star Wars as well. Once that idea was hatched, and it was obvious the main book would be Star Wars, and would follow Luke and the rebels. Darth Vader leading the second book was the natural next step. We followed Anakin's journey as a main character in the prequel trilogy, so it makes sense to keep following him into the original trilogy. There's a side of the character that we didn't know existed when those movies came out, but we had the opportunity to delve into it in a way that ties the two eras closer together.

Jennifer Heddle: When the series was in the concept stage I figured it would just be a fun read about Darth Vader kicking butt across the galaxy—not that there's anything wrong with that! But what Kieron and Salva made became much, much more. I realized by the end of the very first issue that this team was on to something special.

> ## MEET TEAM VADER!
>
> KIERON GILLEN, writer
>
> SALVADOR "SALVA" LARROCA, artist
>
> FRANK PARISI, senior editor, Lucasfilm
>
> JENNIFER HEDDLE, senior editor, Lucasfilm
>
> JORDAN D. WHITE, comics editor, Marvel
>
> HEATHER ANTOS, assistant editor, Marvel

What made Marvel decide Kieron Gillen and Salvador Larroca were the ideal team?

JDW: I thought of Kieron because of his amazing ability to write compelling evil. When Kieron wrote Uncanny X-Men, it was a dark time for the X-Men and, in my opinion, one in which they were close to being super-villains. Even so, he made Cyclops and company very understandable and interesting. In addition, his work on Uber for Avatar Press is literally re-imagining the darkest parts of the 20th century and making them even more horrific, while still telling an engrossing story. Both of those series mixed in my head and made me sure he could get into the mind of the worst villain in the galaxy.

Salva is a huge Star Wars fan; and the moment we got word that we were getting the rights for Star Wars, we knew we had to bring his amazing talent to the Star Wars galaxy. It was just a question of on what title. He's been able to capture the tone of the series so perfectly, from the first scene of issue #1 with Vader striding into Jabba's palace, right up through the last scene of issue #25 with... Oh, people might not have read it yet. I should hold off!

Kieron, how did Darth Vader enter your life? Is it true that you almost turned it down?

Kieron Gillen: One day I picked up the phone and it was Jordan. He asked if I'd be interested in writing the sister book to Jason Aaron's Star Wars. It was something of a surprise.

And yes, it's true I almost turned it down. The prosaic part is simple—I wasn't sure it would fit into my schedule. The more romantic part is that I wasn't sure I was the

THE FORCE IS OBSOLETE. THESE ARE ITS SUCCESSORS.

right man for the job. I was aware that Marvel had a lot of writers who would kill to do it! In the end, I decided I was as qualified as anyone, which is a terrible piece of ego. One of the main criticisms of my work at Marvel is paying more attention than I should to the villains and their motivations, but here that is a positive boon. For that and a bunch of other reasons, I realized maybe I actually was the right person for the job.

Salva, what was your reaction to being offered penciling duties?
Salvador Larroca: Surprise! A year before starting, Marvel told me they wanted me and it was a tremendous joy. But I preferred to be cautious until the scripts were ready. When they confirmed I was definitely going to do it, I was thrilled.

Was _Star Wars_ a big part of both your childhoods?
KG: My first movie experience was seeing _The Empire Strikes Back_ in the cinema. It was my entry into pop-fantasy culture; and Darth Vader was my first iconic image of evil. That I get to write the prequel to my own introduction to this world that could blow a few fuses if you consider it too long!
SL: Yes, of course. I saw the movies as a child and I've always been a great fan.

I've always been fascinated by the character of Darth Vader. I'm afraid I've always gone with the villains! It is always more fun to draw villains than heroes—though in our story the Dark Lord is the hero, really.

What was your vision for the series at the start?
KG: When Jordan called it wasn't definitely a Darth Vader book. He told me if I had a better idea, go for it... But it was never _not_ going to be Vader for me.

I viewed it almost like a historical novel because it's set in a distinct period in the saga. At the end of _A New Hope_, Vader is one of the few survivors to one of the biggest military disasters of all time, and he's at least partially to blame. But at the start of _Empire_, he's commanding the fleet, killing people at will, and generally has more power than ever. There's an implied story there—the fall and rise of Darth Vader—and that's what my arc would be.

The second key element, and the real emotional meat, is that between the two movies Vader realizes that he has a son. He realizes that the last 20 years of his life have been a lie. We had to do the inversion of the "I Am Your Father" scene—the "I Have a Son" scene.

I often use [the Netflix political

drama] _House of Cards_ as a shorthand description for the series: A powerful man feels slighted and turns to tactics he may have previously shunned to reach new heights of power. That core vision remained, though the execution always wanders. You knew in your heart of hearts that the final panel of Vader's story would be him, on the bridge of the _Executor_, about to go after Luke.

JDW: It probably won't be _too_ surprising to hear that one of our major touchpoints in talking about what this book would be was [the AMC drama] _Breaking Bad_. Even though the series is heavy with gut-wrenching emotion, it always found room for humor. I think Kieron referred to [the project] as a post-_Breaking Bad_ take on Darth Vader at one point, and I think [he] is very right.

Salva, you've worked with several noted _Star Wars_ scribes. How is Kieron different?
SL: Every writer is different, as every artist is, too. Kieron is very easy to work with because he is very visual in his descriptions. He is a very good writer and his scripts are fun, which is important for an artist. When you spend a lot of time with a story, you have to have fun with it, otherwise it becomes very hard.

Kieron, were you ever nervous pitching Lucasfilm some of your more... inventive ideas?

KG: Generally speaking, we had a "Don't self-censor" approach. Don't assume that Lucasfilm will say no; pitch it and let them say no if they want to. We wanted to test where the limits were, but we were never going to pitch anything that wasn't *Star Wars*. For me, *Star Wars* is very much in the space-fantasy mode. It's never been hardcore sci-fi, and that's its charm.

Characters such as the Mon Calamari cyborg Karbin have that wonderful "space fantasy" feel to them. What inspires these characters?

KG: I was trying to think of powerful archetypes that would work in the high-adventure mode that *Star Wars* runs on. That's where we get people like Aphra—fundamentally an ethically inverted Indiana Jones archetype—and Thanoth—basically the genius detective archetype,

but an Empire loyalist. *Star Wars* is about these big, powerful characters, and finding novel ones is a big part of it for me.

Jen and Jordan, did any of Kieron's pitches stand out as especially playful or inventive?

JH: The first thing that comes to mind is the mental image I got when I read Kieron's script about the Geonosian queen being hooked up to an egg-laying machine: "Only her top part is flesh. The entire bottom half of her—the whole reproductive organ—has been replaced by a machine. It is basically the same shape as the organs would have been, but is clearly a machine. At the bottom, it has an egg-laying nozzle, but it's mechanical." I'm not sure "playful" is the word I would use to describe this, but it certainly is inventive! The suggestion of Triple-Zero as essentially a murderous C-3PO was also one of my favorite things. I knew it would work really beautifully and that fans would love it.

JDW: To me, the greatest and most joyful surprise was all the new and charming characters that grew in the series. From the beginning, it was clear that Kieron understood the Dark Lord and had great plans for him. But all the new characters came to life on the page in such awesome and surprising ways. Doctor Aphra, Inspector Thanoth, Triple-Zero... They all became such compelling additions to the universe. In retrospect, I am pretty surprise we got away with making the evil R2 and C-3PO. They are actively psychopathic! It's pretty outrageous, but it seems like everyone at Lucasfilm loves them as much as we do, which is amazing.

Heather Antos: The new additions to the *Star Wars* cast have by far been the most pleasing surprise that any editor, creator, or reader could have. Kieron, Salva, and colorist Edgar Delgado's ability to bring suc life to them has been astonishing to say the least. They've only been around for just

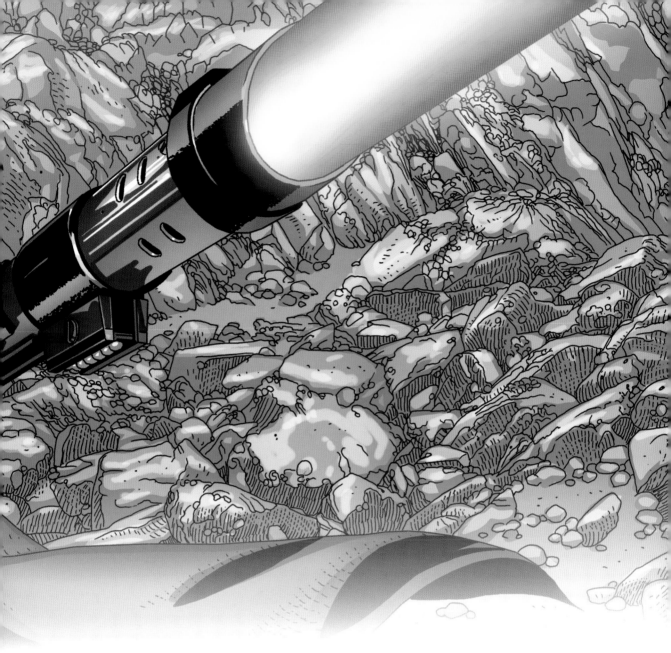

der two years, but I now can't imagine the
ar Wars universe without them!

Issue #24 has one of my all-time favorite
arth Vader moments, and one that I was
ocked we were allowed to do. It's a battle
tween Darth Vader and his former self,
akin. Of course, it all takes place in
der's head, but the fact that we get to see
der's perspective on what went down on
ustafar—however skewed that perspective
ay have been—was super cool to do!

lva, who were your favorite characters
draw, other than Vader?
.: I love Aphra. She is special for me.
d Cylo of course, because it's me!

eron, what's your process in scripting
issue? What makes writing Star Wars
fferent from other Marvel titles like
or or Iron Man?
G: It's Star Wars. That sounds like I'm
king, but that is the key difference, and
anges everything. I had spent basically

the previous six years writing in the Marvel
Universe. Though the Marvel Universe
is a place with a large variety of tones, it
still has a characteristic timbre. Star Wars
has its own mode, and it's different. It's
also narrower—which I don't mean as a
criticism. Our aesthetic goal was always
"We're not doing a comic adaptation of
Star Wars, but we're doing Star Wars on
paper." When looking at my choices when
scripting it's always through the filter
of "Is this evoking what we see on the
screen? Is this Star Wars-y enough?"

In terms of the actual process, it's
similar. I work on a script every day until
it's done; I then leave it in a drawer for a
bit before polishing it later. The secondary
stage is when I hand it into Marvel, who
then passes it to Lucasfilm for approval.
The relationship there also changed
things, and they've been generous with
ideas and resources. At Marvel, I tend to
write in a hermetically sealed way. For
Darth Vader, there have been moments

when I've written in the script: "I can
invent a new crime lord here for this role,
but if there's anyone in this area of the
universe you're using elsewhere,
I can use them instead." Leaning into the
interconnectivity was a characteristic
element of the job.

Also when writing for Marvel I'm less
likely to stomp around the house, pretending
I'm breathing through a ventilator!

What does an artist like Salvador Larroca
bring to a panel? Did he find things in your
writing or storytelling you didn't notice?
KG: Salva is a monster. My friend Matt
Fraction and he collaborated on their
award-winning Iron Man run, so I'd seen
Salva's work extensively before—and also
knew about his blistering speed. That last
attribute is the easiest thing to overlook.
He illustrated the entire Darth Vader
series, thus ensuring the book's visual
consistency. It's easier to lose yourself in
a world like that.

I could see much of what made him perfect in the *Iron Man* run: he does brilliant technology, both in terms of drawing it and designing it. Aphra's *Ark Angel* ship has a great *Star Wars*-feeling design that's not based on anything in-universe. He also does fantastic likenesses, which is obviously a boon when doing *Star Wars*. All that was stuff I hoped for, and he completely delivered. Plus, he's an enormous *Star Wars* fan, which screams from every page.

Probably the most unexpected thing he brought to the page was basing Cylo's likeness on himself. It must have been an odd day at work drawing Darth Vader killing him over and over! It's probably a metaphor for working on the book.

Salva, how did you and Gillen collaborate? Might your pencils have inspired new directions in the story?
SL: I don't know if my drawings have been able to inspire Kieron, I just hope he's as happy with my work as I am with his.

When you work with such a good script, your obligation is to give the best of yourself to maintain quality. Kieron's scripts have been excellent and I tried to work as best as I know. When it's easy to work with someone, a symbiosis occurs, and that is visible in the result. I think that is what happened to us.

I got inspiration only from the movies, and it is important to the fans that the comic characters are recognizable.

Can you describe the challenge of illustrating emotion for a main character encased in black armor and a mask?
SL: I do it with body expression and camera angles. It's a trick that is used in films, too. It is not the first time I have to deal with a character like this. Think of *Iron Man*, for example.

Kieron, you've previously said that Darth Vader was your first image of "evil," since *The Empire Strikes Back* was the first film you saw in a cinema as a kid. How did you keep Vader evil, yet also sympathetic enough for readers to follow him through the series?
KG: It was tricky working out how to present him without getting too close—and losing the essential mystique. That

was something I worried about a lot. Our main solution was to show flashes of his inner life, but only at a distance. You'll have these single panels where you see a memory, but you can never be sure what the memory actually means to Vader. Plus, Salva and I really worked the "Silent panel of Vader staring into distance" hard.

In terms of maintaining sympathy, there were two main lines of attack. Partially it's that the story circles around Vader, and in some ways it's not *him* we're afraid of, but rather everyone around him. Have people we worry about near him definitely helps there—Aphra is key to the book.

The other line is the absolute opposite: by surrounding him with people who are

worse than him. Robert McKee argues in his book *Story* about *The Godfather* that one of the reasons the narrative works is that while the Godfather is monstrous, he's still a better option than anyone else. People find themselves thinking, *If I was a Mafia Godfather, that's the sort of Mafia Godfather I'd want to be.* I definitely did that. Vader is bad, but Grand General Tagge is bad *and* tedious. At least Vader wouldn't corner you in a party and talk to you about his favorite graphs.

I [also] knew the book needed a variety of antagonists. If [the story] solely consisted of Vader killing rebels people would quickly lose interest. I mean, isn't it telling that the moments in the saga we all love most are when Vader mercilessly kills one of his fascist subordinates...?

As *Darth Vader* developed over many issues, did the story or the characters go in different directions than originally intended?
KG: Oh yeah. Many have been a delight. When I realized exactly what Thanoth was going to tell Vader, and why it was shocking, it was a real, "Dude! Are you actually going to do that?" moment. I spent considerable time wondering whether there was any way I could save him. Aphra had a bunch of scenes like that, and writing her desperately squirming to try and escape her fate was a joy. She always had an idea, and her scenes with Vader were always alive. That first happened in issue four, when I realized that the first thing Aphra would do upon completing the mission would be to ask, "So ... are you going to kill me now or later?" That unlocked the Vader-Aphra relationship for me.

The *Darth Vader* series also reveals that not every Imperial dies on the Death Star, as once believed. General Tagge returns in a bold new way to become a foil to the Dark Lord. Who made the decision to bring Tagge back into the fold?
JH: Using Tagge was a suggestion from Lucasfilm that came about during a meeting with Kieron early on. We wanted a foil for Vader who would feel like someone with a real weight behind him, someone that the audience would find believable as holding power alongside Vader and being in the Emperor's favor. Using a character from the conference room scene in *A New Hope* felt like the perfect solution. Everyone was excited about it. It was another bonus that Tagge was a character the audience no doubt already found obnoxious from the movie! You wanted to root against him from the start.

Kieron, how was it breaking story with fellow writer Jason Aaron on *Vader Down*, the crossover between *Darth Vader* and the *Star Wars* monthly?
KG: It was a lot of fun. All of this has been I've known Jason ever since he was just starting *Scalped* and I was doing *Phonogram*. Also, we've had some experience in this kind of thing. Some of my fondest times in writing a shared superhero universe occurred when Jason was writing *Wolverine and the X-Men* and I was writing *Uncanny X-Men*. We batted stuff back and forth in a very casual way.

Vader Down was like that, but more so. We'd already done some close back and forth plotting on our first arc, building up towards issue six's "I Have a Son" reveal, but *Vader Down* was on a different scale from that. We had a variety of ideas, and our original thoughts for the series were miles away from where we ended up. It was a process of iteration, working on the synopsis, seeing where the issue breaks landed, and then just writing it. It was agreeably egoless in that way—we didn't even check which issue would be written by whom. As such, both of us got to write key scenes for each other's casts, almost by random. I'm still envious Jason got to write the initial fight between our two casts, though he's envious I got to write other cool stuff, so it evens out!

Why end *Darth Vader* with issue #25?
JDW: From the very beginning, Kieron always said this would be a finite story, that Vader is going through an arc, and that it would only really work if it had a conclusion. I am sure some will say we reached the end too soon, and a part of me might even agree—the part that just wants this team to keep making evil come true forever and always. But in the end, Kieron is right. The ending is an important part of this series, and it's stronger for getting there.

HA: Kieron has always had an ending in mind for the series. There was a story he wanted to tell, and he was able to do it in 25 amazing issues. I definitely wish the series could go on forever, but I think for a single story to have as much impact as this one has it *has* to end, you know?

Kieron, how would you say Vader's changed as a character from the first issue to the final issue?
KG: For me, it's a story of Vader awakening. Vader knows more of the truth now. As I said, he knows he has a son. Before this story the aim was to be the Emperor's fist. He's done that for 20 years. Now, at least consciously, he wants to seduce Luke to the dark side and rule the Empire.

Ironically, for all the darkness, this is a story of a man regaining his hope and his own destiny. It's just a particularly dark form of hope, which has allowed him to act in an even more ruthless way than before.

What were everyone's favorite moments or scenes?
JH: There are so many! The invention of Aphra is obviously a standout—so many of the great moments in the comic derive from her being a fantastic character. I especially loved Aphra teaming up with the bounty hunters to rob the Imperial ship—all with Vader's knowledge. That

was one of the most fun stories for me. I loved the interplay within that group.

And I loved the cat and mouse game between Vader and Thanoth—giving Vader a worthy rival that actually kept me in suspense about who would come out on top! I think one of Kieron's real strengths on this comic has been surrounding one of the most unforgettable fictional characters of all time with other fictional characters whom you will never forget.

JDW: That is so difficult, as this is a series of amazing moments and characters. Right this moment, I will go with the character of Thanoth. He was so smart and interesting... and was a great antagonist for Vader precisely because he

wasn't one. He was ostensibly on Vader side, and it gave that whole second arc such a great layer of suspense—Vader is working with an investigative genius to solve a crime Vader had committed. Loved that. And Thanoth's return was also pitch perfect, if sometime we debated a bit about his final fate. I still hope, someday, we can read a murder mystery novel that takes place on the Death Star with Thanoth tracking down a killer in the Imperial ranks.

HA: Can I pick every moment that happened between issues 1 through 25? *No*? Fine. In that case, my favorite moment was probably when we did the interwoven scenes between *Darth*

HIS TIE'S ARMED WITH FLECTOR SHIELDS! CONCENTRATE YOUR FIRE ON--

AAARRRGGHH!

THIS IS YELLOW SQUAD, COORDINATING FIRE. ALL TORPEDOES ARE LOCKED.

LET'S SEE HIM DEFLECT THIS!

and were very pleased with how it worked. If I had to pick one, while I was proud of the Obi-Wan and Anakin beats, Padmé whispering, "Stay" is one of my favorite panels in the whole book.

The third one... well, I can't pick between all the times that Triple-Zero and Beetee were monstrous and awful. I could probably do a top 10 of all the things the murderbots did. They were a consistent joy. And let's go with Thanoth and Vader's final confrontation. We did a lot of space epic in the book—obviously!—but sometimes all you need is two people in a darkened room.

Now, at its conclusion, how do you think *Darth Vader* stacks up to the other comics you all have worked on?
SL: At the top of my career.

JDW: Honestly, I believe in my heart that this will be remembered as one of the best Vader stories ever told. I think Kieron and Salva did that great a job.

HA: Kieron, Salva, and Edgar poured their hearts out onto these pages, and it really shows. I truly believe people are going to be talking about this series for a very, very long time come. How could they not?

Salva, would you ever take a trip down into the dark side again?
SL: I hope so, but who knows? I'd really love to. If I can, I'd do it.

Is this truly the end for Kieron Gillen and the Dark Lord of the Sith? Who was the master? And who was the apprentice?
KG: You strike me down and I will become more powerful than you can... wait, Darth. No, stay back. Let's talk this through—
←*thud*

Marvel Comics' *Darth Vader* series 1-3 are available now as trade paperbacks.

der issue six and *Star Wars* issue six, hen it was revealed to Vader that the oublesome rebel pilot was really his on, Luke Skywalker. I mean, what an *vesome* moment to reveal. It's such pivotal moment not just for Vader, ut for the entire *Star Wars* story as we ow it!

L: The sequences in which we tell nakin's past, when we make a trospective, based on the movies. at's very cool. And I am very happy e fans have been able to recognize e same Vader from the films in the omics. That is so cool because it's ry easy to mess with such a difficult aracter to draw.

KG: Well, at least one of them would be in the last issue, and I wouldn't want to spoil that. Suffice to say we're really proud of the conclusion. I'm all about the denouement, me.

The first one is, I suspect, the one that would be on anyone's list. The "I Have a Son" scene. Salva paced it beautifully, and it's as iconic as anything that I've had my hand in while writing comics. It's a scene that any *Star Wars* fan would want to see, and I still can't believe I got to do it.

The second one would be issue #24. An issue-long vision quest isn't exactly what you expect this late in the game, but doing Vader's own cave-sequence-on-Dagobah worked shockingly well. We tried to make it mythic, and keep that sort of structure,

┌─**MORE TO SAY**─┐

Follow Jordan D. White on Twitter @crackshot

Find Kieron Gillen at kierongillen.com and on Twitter @kierongillen

Find Michael Kogge at michaelkogge. com and on Twitter @michaelkogge

Follow Salvador Larroca on Twitter @SalvadorLarroca

Follow Heather Antos on Twitter @HeatherAntos

Follow Jennifer Heddle on Twitter @jenheddle

└─**HAVE YOU?**─┘

ANTHONY DANIELS **ON THE PERILS OF PLAYING C-3PO!**

STAR WARS

REVENGE OF THE SITH!

We Celebrate the 10th Anniversary of Episode III

ISSUE #157
US $7.99
CAN $9.99
MAY/JUNE 2015

Titan

LORDS OF MISRULE

EXPLORING THE LIGHTER SIDE!

Jeffrey Brown on Finding Good in Darth Vader!

The Emperor and Darth Vader unite in an all-new tale—inside!

ORIENTATION
BY JOHN JACKSON MILLER

ISSUE 157
MAY/JUNE 2015

Publishing stories that are part of *Star Wars* canon will always be one of the joys of editing *Star Wars Insider*, but having a story written by much-loved author John Jackson Miller that features not one, but two Sith Lords is a real honor! This tale, featuring Darth Vader and the Emperor as they carry out a surprise inspection, is every bit as tense and exciting as you might expect. There's even an appearance by Miller's Admiral Rae Sloane—a key figure in his *Star Wars* literature since *A New Dawn* in 1994!**—Jonathan Wilkins**

John Jackson Miller was born on January 12, 1968. He is an acclaimed science-fiction author, comic-book writer, and commentator who is also known for his research into comic-book circulation history in the Standard Catalog of Comic Books *series.*

"ORIENTATION"

AN EXCLUSIVE SHORT STORY BY JOHN JACKSON MILLER
WITH ART BY BRIAN ROOD

Battle stations! Hostiles off the starboard bow!"
In the command well of the Imperial cruiser *Defiance*, 20 members of the skeleton crew hastily turned to their terminals, ready to defend against ▮ack. Every mind was attuned to the situation—save the ▮e belonging to the figure looming dark and large above them ▮ the catwalk. Darth Vader looked on with utter disinterest.

There was nothing in this "battle" to engage the Dark Lord's ▮tention. It wasn't real. There was no one to challenge the ▮npire. He and his Master Darth Sidious, who now ruled the ▮laxy as the Emperor, had brought the Clone Wars to a ▮nclusion not long before; and while the two were on their ▮ay to Ryloth now to root out insurgency, the "hostiles" ▮tside were pure fiction, part of a training exercise.

"Hard about, my cretins," shouted Commandant Baylo, ▮ssing Vader as he stalked along the catwalk. "While I've ▮en waiting for your picnic to end, you've lost your forward ▮ields!" He clapped his hands on the railing and leaned over ▮ bellow. "We have an observer today. Are you trying to make ▮e look bad?"

Vader thought he already did. Well past ▮ and with a nose too long for his face, Pell ▮aylo walked with an exaggerated ▮np that caused the stumpy man to ▮b up and down like a flying thing. ▮e nonetheless commanded the ▮tention of the cadets in the pits on ▮ther side of the catwalk, all of ▮hom were now scrambling to ▮rrect their errors.

Vader thought his own presence ▮re was a mistake, too. But Sidious ▮d brought him to *Defiance*'s bridge ▮d left him. It was his duty to ▮main, even if he saw no other ▮ason for being there.

Crossing the vast swath of cosmos ▮tween Coruscant and Ryloth, Darth ▮dious had ordered a stop in the Denon ▮stem so he could consult with several chiefs ▮ the navy, visiting there to discuss how the jumble ▮ affiliated military schools that had existed under the ▮public might be better integrated into the Imperial ▮ademy. His livelihood under review, Baylo had suggested ▮ timesaving solution: the meeting could take place aboard ▮fiance, the cruiser he'd operated as a flight training school ▮r nearly 50 years. The commandant could show his students ▮ action while they conveyed his Imperial Highness on one leg ▮ his trip.

CROSSING THE VAST SWATH OF COSMOS BETWEEN CORUSCANT AND RYLOTH, DARTH SIDIOUS HAD ORDERED A STOP IN THE DENON SYSTEM SO HE COULD CONSULT WITH SEVERAL CHIEFS OF THE NAVY.

The Emperor had praised Baylo for his suggestion. Vader saw through the offer. *A futile effort to save his school.* The Clone Wars had brought the *Defiance* Flight Training Institute—known to most spacers as "the Baylo School"—directly under the umbrella of the Republic Navy, with Baylo receiving a rank as a line officer. Yet the commandant treated the institute as his personal property, ignoring schedules and asserting he knew best when recruits were ready for service. Even now, with the Empire in charge, naval leaders were loath to rein Baylo in; he'd trained many of them aboard *Defiance*, after all. Vader expected that resistance would wilt, now that the Emperor was on the scene. Baylo was just another fossil, married to archaic practices.

But his Master had spent half a minute on the bridge before departing for his meetings with the naval chiefs who were Baylo's superiors—leaving Vader behind to observe Baylo's silly pantomime show. Vader had objected, as strenuously as he dared: "I would serve you better elsewhere, Master." The Emperor had not been amused. "I decide where you are needed. You will remain and be my eyes."

That was hours ago, and Vader hadn't seen anything worth his attention. Baylo had run his cadets through their paces, dressing down one after another and spewing aphorisms. The first mock attack concluded, he unleashed another one.

"—it's all about attitude, in more ways than one," Baylo was saying to someone, mid-rant. "Think about your direction, your facing. Don't you know where you're going, cadet? Because if *you* don't, your ship certainly won't..."

The trainees—humans in their early twenties, some on their first orientation flights—seemed almost happy to absorb the platitudes and abuse. Vader knew Baylo had a mythic status in naval circles, and not just for his exploits. *Defiance* had fought pirates when it was in patrol service, yes—but Baylo's spine had been injured, and now his daily battle was with near-constant pain. Twice since he had been aboard, Vader had heard cadets whispering of Baylo's bravery in working despite the agony. *Ridiculous.* Baylo knew nothing of pain.

A voice came from behind. "Shuttle arriving from Denon, Commandant. Vice Admiral Tallatz aboard."

Baylo stood back from the railing. "That'll be the last of Palpatine's—of the *Emperor's* guests for his meeting." He checked the time. "Navigator, plot our hyperspace route to—"

"I already have it, sir," called out a female voice from the pit.

"I'll be the judge of that." Forcing one atrophied foot in front of the other, Baylo fought his way down the steps into the command well. A woman with deep brown skin, dressed in sharp cadet grays, slid her chair from her terminal, allowing the old man to approach. She wore the trace of a knowing smile as Baylo read the monitor.

"I'm impressed, cadet," he said. "You'll go far—and so will this ship. Or did you *not* intend to plot a course into Wild Space?"

The cadet's grin vanished. The young woman looked past him at her calculations, suddenly puzzled. "It is a course to Christophsis, sir, where the *Perilous* will meet us."

"You've failed to account for a singularity along our route which will reshape our hyperspace passage in a most startling way. We now know who our next admiral will be," he added with a snort. The young woman stepped away in humiliation as Baylo began to work the console. After a moment's effort, he stepped back. "There. Small repair, major difference." He looked around and about. "Details matter, everyone. A navy isn't built on captains—but on crews that watch their work."

"Aye, Commandant," came the response from the cadets.

Aware of Vader's gaze, Baylo looked up at the Dark Lord. "They don't learn right away, but they do learn. I get results. You can tell your Emperor that."

"He is your Emperor, as well." They were the first words Vader had spoken before the trainees, and several shifted in their seats on hearing his powerful voice.

But if Baylo was shaken, he didn't show it. "I'm sorry. I forget—what are you to the Emperor, again?"

"You would do well never to learn."

That time, Vader got a reaction. Baylo straightened—a strenuous feat for him—and he slapped the back of the chair of the woman he had corrected. "Well, I can still teach my people a few things. Extra courier detail for you, Sloane, once you're done here. You can think about navigation while you're finding your way around ship."

"Aye, Commandant." The cadet returned to her station and stared blankly at the screen before her, trying to understand her mistake.

Baylo hobbled back toward the staircase. "You have the settings. Take us to hyperspace as soon as the admiral's docking is complete. I need to prepare in case they need me." He struggled up the steps and made his way past Vader. "Carry on, cadets."

Vader watched the aged commandant exit—and then thought about the exchange. The man Vader had been would have bristled at such treatment. His Jedi teachers all thought they knew better than he did. And they were so smug, always pretending they knew some secret about the universe he was unworthy to learn. It was all a lie, a false front to hide their weaknesses. Darth Sidious, now the Emperor, had the secrets, not them. It had been a delight to prove them all wrong.

But Sidious was now in that same role as teacher, and he was doing many of the same things: acting as though he knew better, and doling out information only as he chose. Vader had traded all the masters on the Jedi council for one. A better one, he knew: the secrets of power Sidious shared were real. And yet, as different as their master-apprentice relationship was, he had served Sidious long enough to get that familiar feeling. The Emperor had something else to do—and he had given Vader busy work.

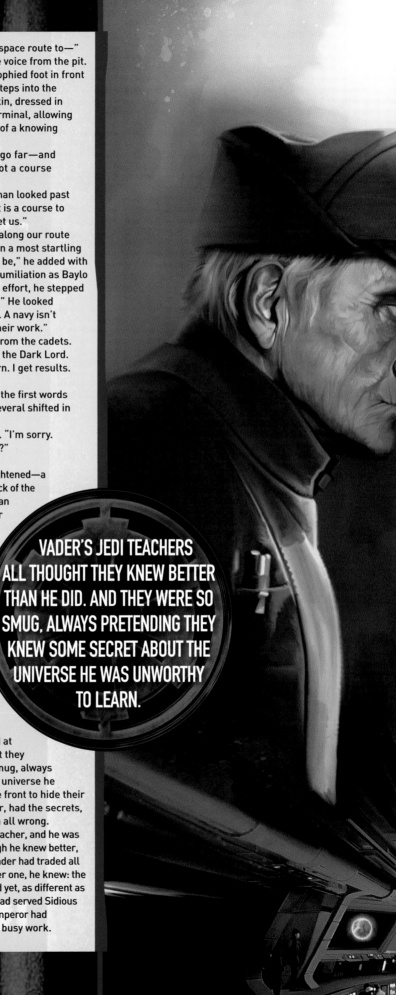

VADER'S JEDI TEACHERS ALL THOUGHT THEY KNEW BETTER THAN HE DID. AND THEY WERE SO SMUG, ALWAYS PRETENDING THEY KNEW SOME SECRET ABOUT THE UNIVERSE HE WAS UNWORTHY TO LEARN.

No. That concept fundamentally clashed with something Vader had long known about himself. *Every job I do is important—because I am the one doing it.*

His cape trailing behind him, Vader descended the stairs into the command well. There, at the end, sat the chastened cadet from earlier.

"Tallatz has debarked," called out her neighbor. "His shuttle's clear."

Sloane looked hard at the numbers before her again and sighed. "Commandant's coordinates locked in the navicomputer. Stand by for hyperspace jump on my mark."

"*Hold.*"

Vader's voice startled her, and she turned her chair. Brown eyes widened as she looked up at him. "Yes, my lord?"

"What do you see?"

"N-nothing."

"You fear to contradict your master."

She shuffled in her seat. "My lord, I don't wish to say the admiral is wrong about—"

"No. That is *exactly* what you wish to do." The woman had hidden her emotions from her companions, but could not fool Vader. He had felt her anger at being embarrassed—and it had bubbled up since, finally breaking through his own preoccupied thoughts. "Speak, cadet—?"

"Sloane." She swallowed hard. "Rae Sloane, of Ganthel." She gestured to the panel behind her. "I've studied our orientation and done the math, with the computer and without. Something isn't right..."

Baylo was waiting in the anteroom as Vader stepped onto the administrative deck. Wearing an antique greatcoat, dress attire for the era during which he trained, Baylo leaned near a large viewport looking out upon the streaming stars of hyperspace. He was using the window frame for support, Vader saw. He looked old, even for Baylo.

He straightened as he saw Vader. "Told you we'd get underway on time."

Vader said nothing.

"Hmph." Baylo looked back at the closed door. "Not used to waiting outside my own office."

"It is not your office."

Baylo looked at Vader—and chuckled lightly. "Whatever you say," he said. Before the old man could return his gaze outside, the door to the office opened. Three women and one man emerged, admirals all: chiefs of various branches of the Imperial Navy. Each glanced briefly at Baylo and silently headed for the elevator.

That evoked a frown from the commandant, but only for a moment. "The Emperor will see us now," Vader said.

"Who told you that?"

Vader simply pointed to the door. Shrugging, Baylo took a breath and started for it, shadowed by the Dark Lord.

The master of *Defiance* stood in his own office, hands clasped and eyes directly forward. The room was windowless save for a single viewport—and the walls were covered with plaques and pictures depicting the names and faces of cadet classes from the past. Vader thought the room somber, a pathetic shrine to a soon-to-be-forgotten past. An appropriate setting, too: seated at Baylo's desk, the black-robed Emperor began to describe his just-settled plans for the Imperial Academy. They included several modifications to streamline operations, making the body more responsive to him. And one other change: "*Defiance* is approaching obsolescence—and we will employ no one who is unresponsive to command. The 'Baylo

School', as you call it, will be folded into the existing training center at Corellia. And you will take a chair at the navigation institute planetside."

"No."

The Emperor was more surprised by Baylo's response than Vader was. "Repeat yourself," his Master said, in a voice nearing a hiss.

"No, I will not transfer this vessel to your new command." Still standing as erect as his gnarled frame would allow, Baylo nodded toward the great seal on the wall to the right of his desk. *Defiance* was commissioned by the Galactic Republic—and detached to me so those who trained here might serve that Republic. I do not recognize your order as legitimate."

The Emperor frowned. "Don't play games, Commandant. Whether you've had time to redecorate or not, the Republic is no more. The Senate decided—"

"—to dissolve its pact with the people," Baylo said, voice rising in volume. "What I owed allegiance to no longer exists. I consider the Galactic Empire a hostile power—and I can't fulfill these orders." He reached inside his waistcoat, an act that drew Vader's immediate attention. But before he reached through the Force to summon his lightsaber, Vader saw Baylo produce a datapad. "This is my resignation." He offered it to the Emperor.

The Emperor simply stared. Then he chuckled. "A republican, Baylo? I was told you were more intelligent."

Finding no takers, Baylo returned the datapad to his pocket. "I am, of course, willing to report to the brig until we reach our destination. I understand the need to keep an orderly ship." He fixed his eyes on the Emperor. "But order's place is in the military. Not in civilian life." Baylo looked back toward Vader. Seeing no response, the commandant shrugged. He looked up

> **VADER TOOK A STEP TOWARD BAYLO. HE, TOO, HAD BEEN WATCHING THE STARS FLYING PAST OUTSIDE WHILE LISTENING TO THE MAN'S LITTLE SPEECH—AND WAITING TO SEE HOW THE EMPEROR WOULD REACT.**

to the viewport, and the stars streaking by. "Enjoy the rest of your journey. I figure I'm dismissed."

Vader took a step toward Baylo. He, too, had been watching the stars flying past outside while listening to the man's little speech—and waiting to see how the Emperor reacted. Baylo turned to discover Vader barring his way. "This guy again." Baylo spoke through clenched teeth, trying not to betray any fear. "I don't care if you kill me."

"No," Vader said. *That much is true.*

"Because you think you are already dead."

The Emperor looked keenly at Vader.

"His ailments?"

"No. He plotted a course that will cause *Defiance* to emerge from hyperspace at Christophsis—and plunge into the sun."

The Emperor's eyes widened a little.

"I countermanded the orders."

Now they narrowed. His Master asked, "And?"

And as if in answer, *Defiance* returned to realspace at that moment—with millions of safe kilometers between it and the aforementioned star. Vader could see it shining outside the viewport, along with something else: *Perilous* was there, waiting as instructed.

Seeing them, Baylo mouthed an obscenity. The Emperor saw them, too. "Very good, my old friend." He looked kindly on Vader. "This is part of what I expect from you—to manage the petty problems so that I can focus on larger matters."

Vader felt a surge of pride. He had suspected it was a test the Emperor had placed in his path; instead, he'd caught something his Master had missed. Even so, the word "petty" didn't sit well with Vader, and he could feel it bothered Baylo more. "You have something to say?" Vader asked.

"You bet," Baylo said, throwing caution away. He'd sagged

learning of his
…ot's failure, but
…focusing his pain
…d anger on the
…mperor he seemed
…gain strength.
…'ve watched you
…d your cronies,
…lpatine. Corrupting
…e navy, bit by bit
…ring the Clone
…ars. Turning
…mething noble,
…mething meant
…a shield, into a
…eapon. Something
…pressive. A
…rvice it's taken
…enerations to build,
…at students of
…ine have given
…eir lives to!" He
…rust his finger to
…e images on the
…r wall. "I'm older
…an you, 'Emperor'—
…o matter what
…u look like now.
…emember
…hen this was an
…norable calling!"

Vader had been
…aiting for his
…aster's angry
…eprisal ever since
…aylo opened his
…srespectful mouth, but instead the Emperor
…eemed amused. "You would have killed several of your
…wn colleagues."

"Traitors, trying to save their posts."

"And a crew of your cadets, for vengeance?"

"A better fate than turning them into droids. Because
…at's what you want, isn't it? Mindless slaves, just robots
…your—"

The words caught in Baylo's throat—as did his breath. Vader
…utched the fingers of his right hand together, summoning the
…ark side of the Force to snap the commandant's windpipe. He
…ll to the deck like a Toydarian whose wings had been clipped;
…not unpleasant comparison, Vader thought.

But the Emperor's smile vanished. "Lord Vader!" he said,
…sing from his seat. "I did not instruct you to kill him."

Vader looked at the Emperor and said nothing. Alone
…gain, they were master and apprentice, Sidious and Vader:
…nd the elder Sith Lord spoke freely and angrily. "I would
…ave kept the wretch alive, to take pleasure from his pain as
…ransformed his Navy—while I broke down his precious ship
…to cafeteria trays." He mused as he looked on the corpse.
…nd a teacher who could so easily kill his students might be
…olded into something I could use."

"He was a threat," Vader said. "He is finished."

Sidious scowled. "Still, I did not command it."

"He is a petty thing, one of those you expect *me* to deal
…ith. My way is faster," Vader said, before catching himself,
…nd adding: "—Master."

Sidious looked at him. But before more words could
…ass between them, a chime came from the door. "Enter,"
…e Emperor said.

The door slid
open, and Sloane
stepped forward.
"Captain Luitt of
Perilous has hailed,"
she said. Reluctant
to look directly at
the Emperor and
his ominous servant,
she sought for
something else
to focus on. "He's
ready to resume
your journey to
Ryloth as soon as
you…" The proper
cadet trailed off as
her eyes discovered
the body on the floor.
She gasped.

"Commandant
Baylo succumbed
to his injuries at
last," the Emperor
said, indifferent.

Sloane looked
startled. Baylo had
been all right the
last time she'd seen
him. But she could
not be unhappy,
Vader thought: Baylo
had belittled her in
public. Sloane would
probably realize that
later, once she
remembered where her priorities lay. She was smart, and
smart people could figure that out.

But now the Emperor claimed her attention as he stepped
past the fallen commandant en route to the exit. "I have an
additional instruction for you to convey to your superiors at
the Academy."

"Y-yes, my lord?"

"This training vessel's name is to be changed," the Emperor
said, looking back purposefully at Vader. "From *Defiance*—
to *Obedience*."

"Of—of course." She bowed and prepared to follow.

And Vader did, as well.

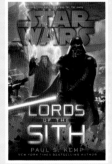

MORE TO SAY

The Emperor and Darth Vader's
journey continues in *Star Wars:
Lords of the Sith* by Paul S. Kemp,
from Del Rey.

HAVE YOU?

John Jackson Miller is the *New York Times* bestselling author
of *Star Wars: Kenobi*, *Star Wars: Lost Tribe of the Sith*, and *Star
Wars: Knight Errant*. His most recent novel, *Star Wars: A New
Dawn* is out now in paperback. His website is farawaypress.
com, and he can be found on Twitter at @jjmfaraway.

THE FIRST ORDER **COLLECTORS' COVER**

CHOOSE YOUR SIDE: ARE YOU WITH THE FIRST ORDER OR THE RESISTANCE?

STAR WARS

THE FORCE AWAKENS

WARS

INSIDER

FEATURING

HARRISON FORD
CARRIE FISHER
ANTHONY DANIELS
PETER MAYHEW
DAISY RIDLEY
OSCAR ISAAC
JOHN BOYEGA
LUPITA NYONG'O
ADAM DRIVER
GWENDOLINE CHRISTIE
DOMHNALL GLEESON
J.J. ABRAMS
AND MORE!

ISSUE #162
US $7.99
CAN $9.99
JAN 2016

TITAN

ADAM DRIVER
KYLO REN

ISSUE 162
JANUARY 2016

The question of how to follow up Darth Vader as *Star Wars'* foremost villain is one I'm pleased I didn't have to answer! Iconic in every aspect, it seemed there was no way to replace the Dark Lord in our hearts. However, Adam Driver's conflicted Kylo Ren could well prove every bit the icon Vader was. His distinctive mask and hood have an emotionless menace to them, the modulated voice sounds genuinely terrifying, and the lightsaber is as unique and seemingly unstable as its owner; and that instability is perfectly captured by Adam Driver, who succeeds in conveying Ren's rage-filled tantrums without sacrificing the character's impressive strength. Despite the satisfyingly familiar trappings of villainy, this emotional turmoil singles out Ren—or should we say Ben?—as a very different kind of *Star Wars* bad guy.
—Jonathan Wilkins

Adam Douglas Driver was born on November 19, 1983. He came to prominence as Adam Sackler in the HBO comedy-drama series Girls*—for which he received three consecutive Primetime Emmy award nominations—before winning worldwide acclaim as Kylo Ren in* Star Wars: The Force Awakens *in 2015.*

ADAM DRIVER IS
KYLO REN

E MYSTERIOUS KYLO REN, AS PLAYED BY ADAM DRIVER, MENACES OUR HEROES
STAR WARS: THE FORCE AWAKENS

Star Wars Insider: How did you get involved with The Force Awakens?

Adam Driver: I think it was the last day of shooting *Girls* and I got a phone call to see if I was interested in meeting J.J. Abrams to talk about *Star Wars*. I thought that it would be interesting to do, so I said "yes." A month later, I left for LA and I met J.J. to talk about the role. Then I met with Kathleen Kennedy, who talked more about it. I was very excited. It's such a big thing and I've never done anything quite like this with this many moving pieces. Wearing a mask is quite a challenging thing. It was very scary and terrifying, so it wasn't something that immediately seemed

It was all character—there was hardly any talk of special effects. When we originally met and talked, it was all about grounding these people in a reality, even though it's a long time ago in a galaxy far, far away. If no one cares about what's happening or no one believes that these people are real, then you won't care about any of it.

What sense did you have of taking on such a role?

The idea of doing it is a scary thing. Even though J.J. mapped out what that character does, he left out a lot of things for us to discover. He wanted to get my input, which was a huge thing also in a movie of this scale. Suddenly

"THERE'S SOMETHING EMPOWERING FOR SOMEONE TO COMPLETELY HIDE THEMSELVES IN A MASK THAT IS SO INTIMIDATING."

like a "yes." Actually, I thought about it quite a bit, even though it was kind of a no-brainer, but I didn't want to take it lightly.

How much was J.J. Abrams able to share with you after you signed on?

J.J. Abrams pretty much walked me through the whole thing. He talked about how he wanted to start it and the themes that he was going with. He talked about things that inspired him that he and Lawrence Kasdan were already working on. There have been small changes since then, but it's all pretty much the same. J.J. had ideas that were very clear in his mind about the conventions that he wanted to upturn and things that grounded Kylo Ren as a character. Character was something that he talked about the most. I feel like some of the movies are so heavy on special effects or visuals and lot of things get lost as far as two people talking to one another. And that was something that J.J. stressed from the beginning;

you have a director who wants you to be involved in making it, and given the history of these movies, that's very exciting. I was a fan of the *Star Wars* movies when I was younger, so suddenly to work on it in my adult life and have input seems unbelievable.

Did you enjoy working on practical sets?

Everything is so real. I think grounding everything in a reality is more effective. Not to get on a high horse about technology, but sometimes it's in place of something that's real and tactile and I think that people take it for granted.

I've actually read the *Making of Star Wars*, and learning how all those people were doing things out of this need to do something different. The conventional way of making a movie at that time and special effects were very important, but it was all about people collaborating in a room together trying to figure out a way to make it real.

As an actor, is it freeing or limiting to wear the mask?
It's both. I get here for three or four days to shoot, and I put all this stuff on, the mask and the costume, then I put it away for a few weeks. Then I come back to it. It was such an evolving thing up until the days we started working on it. Then you're thrown into it, and boom! Then suddenly I can't see the ground. They are all good challenges. As we've been shooting, I find it more freeing. The physical life is really important. There are so many layers to him anyway. It's interesting to find out who he is with the mask on or with the mask off, and that was part of our initial conversations. There's something empowering for someone to completely hide themselves in a mask that is so intimidating.

Did you talk to J.J. Abrams and costume designer Michael Kaplan about the look of Kylo Ren at all?
It was such an evolving thing. I'd fly in to see what they were coming up with and see nods to Akira Kurosawa, and his jacket that bows out just a little bit, like a samurai, and all those references. Then I'd leave for two weeks and come back to see how it was shaped a little more. My only input was whether it felt good or bad. I was involved in making it functional, which was great. They were all about how they could make it more efficient and something that someone could wear. It looks great, but if you can't move in it or breathe in it, then it doesn't make sense for the audience or the actor.

How did you go about conveying the character's physicality?
Trying to convey someone whose physical life is very much about combat and fighting in a short amount of time is a challenging thing. One of the first things I wanted to do, as soon as everything was all scheduled, was to start drilling daily and making it part of my daily life. I had three months to prepare, so I wanted to immerse myself in the training as much as possible. The first week was like four hours a day of fight training; just stretching and going over the training with sticks

ckwise, from
t: Early concept
showing Kylo
's helmet in
ail; more concept
showing Kylo Ren
a rare, reflective
od; poised for
on!

"I'D FLY IN TO SEE WHAT THEY WERE COMING
UP WITH AND SEE NODS TO AKIRA KUROSAWA,
AND HIS JACKET THAT BOWS OUT A BIT,
LIKE A SAMURAI."

d slowly building up to the lightsaber.
en I went to New York and worked with
ople they sent there. Whenever we're
t on set, I'm always with the fight guys.
s almost like a play in a way, the dancing
rt of fighting. There's a structure and
s important to know where everything's
ing. You always learn new things about
and for me this has been a process
here a lot of the external things have
en formed that gave me more
formation. Usually I feel like I try to
ork internally and try to think about
w it feels from the inside out, but for
is there are so many tactile things that
an actually hold on to that give me a lot
information. The fight choreography
as one of them.

Vas the table read a surreal experience?
eeing everybody all in one room for the
ble read was surreal; I just wanted to
t back as an audience member and listen
them. I remember in the read-through
at things would just come to life when

the original characters read their
parts. Suddenly I just wanted to sit back
and watch and enjoy the movie, but
then I realized I had lines to say
and a part to play. I got to act
across from people who have no
idea that they are very much a part
of my youth.

What makes Star Wars great?
At the end of it, I think the great
thing about Star Wars is that,
yes, it's a long time ago in a
galaxy far, far away and there are
spaceships and lightsabers, but the
family story and the friendship and
sacrifice elements are really big,
human themes that make it enduring.
All those human things are what
connected people to those movies
in the first place. It's never been
taken lightly, and there's always
been a conversation that starts
with putting the humanity
in it. ✦

BOBA FETT: THE ANIMATED ORIGIN OF THE SAGA'S MOST **ENIGMATIC BAD GUY!**

STAR WARS
INSIDER
®

THE FORCE AWAKENS
Adapting the hit movie
into a hit novel!

TAKE A WALK ON THE DARK SIDE!
INSIDER REVEALS WHY KYLO REN IS A GREAT *STAR WARS* VILLAIN!

ISSUE #164
US $7.99
CAN $9.99
APRIL 2016

TITAN

KYLO REN
THE POWER OF THE DARK SIDE

ISSUE 164
APRIL 2016

One of the great joys of being a *Star Wars* fan is that new material always provokes lively discussion. The release of *The Force Awakens* was no exception, with much of the focus being on Kylo Ren. It seemed worthwhile for *Insider* to get some notable *Star Wars* experts to add their thoughts to the mix, and to explore why Ren is such an effective presence in the movie. As ever, the great and the good had plenty to say, with authors and commentators keen to share what they thought made a good villain, and how Kylo Ren stacks up alongside his eminent predecessors.—**Jonathan Wilkins**

WHY THE *STAR WARS*
SAGA'S NEWEST BAD GUY
IS ALSO THE MOST DANGEROUS.
WORDS: BRYAN YOUNG

"Villains have been so important in film history," Roger Ebert once said, "you could almost argue there wouldn't be movies without them. Film is the most dynamic storytelling known to man and it lends itself to melodrama and conflict: good guys versus bad guys." And of *Star Wars* specifically, he said that, "each film is only as good as its villain."

It's hard to argue with a man held as the gold standard of film criticism, and it's through this lens we'll be taking a look at Kylo Ren and what he adds to *Star Wars: The Force Awakens*.

Through the entire classic saga, the heroes of the Republic, then the Rebellion, are plagued by the phantom menace, Darth Sidious, and his grand plan for the Sith. Along the way he had some of the most fearsome right hands of doom, from Darth Maul and Count Dooku to General Grievous before finally settling on the worst of them all: Darth Vader. Each of these villains were some of the best

THE POWER OF THE DARK SIDE: KYLO REN

to grace the silver screen, but the shadow of Darth Vader looms large in the newest installment of the Skywalker saga of *Star Wars* films.

We talked to a number of *Star Wars* experts about what they think makes a great villain and how Kylo Ren stacks up to this standard.

Paul S. Kemp is the author of *Lords of the Sith*, which made him a logical first choice to turn to:

"A great villain is one whose villainy makes sense, whose drives are understandable, even if not sympathetic. We don't know all of Kylo's backstory, but he appears in some ways to have been a failure, as both an aspiring Jedi and perhaps also as a son. That sense of failure and the insecurity it creates festered, and to overcome both he turned to Vader, who—to Kylo—embodied strength, confidence, power, and maybe even served as a kind of proxy father figure since Han, obviously, did not. That's all relatable, right? We can understand that. Of course, emulating Vader doesn't actually fill his emotional holes, so he piles frustration and rage onto his insecurity and *boom*, we've got this emotionally rich character who vacillates between a rage-filled teenager and a frightening would-be Sith Lord. He's a character on the edge—or the bridge, if you prefer—and we're watching his formative years.

I found even the small glimpse of him we got in the film to be a fascinating one."

Holly Frey is the host of the top-rated podcast *Stuff You Missed in History Class*, but is also an intense *Star Wars* fan who writes for *StarWars.com*:

"To me, the ingredients for making a great villain are: intensity, style, charisma, unpredictability, and a steadfast belief that their cause is just.

In Kylo Ren, we're seeing the kernel of a true villain—almost like a villain embryo. He's got all the ingredients, and we're actually getting to see the evil soufflé bake. That makes for an interesting ride, because you don't actually know how it will turn out. Seeing a villain wobble in their development is really compelling.

On a scale of Ozzel to Greedo, both great villains that I love, I'd wager Kylo Ren is somewhere around Bossk, which is high praise indeed."

C. Robert Cargill is a long time film critic, the author of *Dreams and Shadows*, and is the screenwriter of upcoming *Dr. Strange* motion picture for Marvel Studios. Here's his take on Kylo Ren:

"A great villain has to be more than just an obstacle; they have to mean something to the audience, to the story. They have to represent some ideal or philosophy or concept that makes them more than just something we want to see stopped. They have to deepen the story every bit as much as the hero does. The most interesting thing about Kylo Ren is the meta nature of him. Here we have a movie that wants to live up to the legend of a nearly 40 year-old franchise, and in it

"A GREAT VILLAIN HAS TO BE MORE THAN JUST AN OBSTACLE; THEY HAVE TO MEAN SOMETHING TO THE AUDIENCE, TO THE STORY."
—C. ROBERT CARGILL

we have a villain that wants to live up to the legend of the villain in that franchise. Ren is always grasping for that legend, trying to live up to it, worried at every moment that he might not be able to be the man his grandfather was—that he might fail himself, his grandfather, and in a very meta way, us, the audience. It's a bold thematic statement worn on its sleeve and I admire it for that."

Michael A. Stackpole is a legendary name amongst *Star Wars* fans, as he wrote *I, Jedi,* and the first five books of the X-Wing series, among others.

"A good villain is driven, internally consistent, ruthless and remorseless and, for me, elegant. Kylo Ren hits most of those attributes pretty well. I the presentation and I am looking forward to seeing what happens next."

Amy Ratcliffe is a world-renowned expert on *Star Wars*, a fellow contributor to *Star Wars Insider*, and co-host of the *Full of Sith* podcast:

"The most interesting villains are conflicted ones. I want someone who is unsure and pulled between good and bad, light and dark. I'm also fascinated by villains who act based on righteous intentions. That's incredibly dangerous. And Kylo Ren—he is unquestionably torn. He wants to be as cold and ruthless as Darth Vader, but he feels a pull to the light. His emotions, rash behavior, and uncertainty make him fascinating.

Kylo Ren is the villain *Star Wars* needed. In some ways, he's a parallel of Luke. When Luke underwent his training, he was focused on pursuing the light side but he was tempted, albeit briefly, by the dark side. Kylo's dealing

"KYLO REN IS THE VILLAIN *STAR WARS* NEEDED. IN SOME WAYS, HE'S A PARALLEL OF LUKE." —AMY RATCLIFFE

with the opposite, and it makes him a formidable threat, and more nuanced than the villains who have come before him. In the scene when Kylo kills his father, I tear up first when Kylo says, 'I'm being torn apart.' His emotion is so raw. I've never felt that from another villain in *Star Wars*."

As the author of *Aftermath*, the first book bridging the divide between *Return of the Jedi* and *The Force Awakens*, Chuck Wendig wouldn't let us *not* take his opinion on Kylo Ren's villainy:

"For me, a villain at the surface has to be cool and has to be scary, right? Like, you need someone who is a real bad news kind of character, someone who enters the scene and, with presence, lets you feel awe in the truest sense of the word. But that's not really enough, to me. You have to go deeper, you have to have a villain who has more going on—remember, villains don't know they're the villains. They think they're the heroes! They are the protagonists of their own story. Vader is great when he first steps onto the *Tantive IV*, but he gets

> **"A GREAT VILLAIN IS THE SORT THAT CAN HAVE A CONVERSATION WITH THE HERO, BECAUSE YOU KNOW IT'S GOING TO BE A FASCINATING CONVERSATION."**
> **—CHUCK WENDIG**

really interesting with *The Empire Strikes Back* when you learn that he's—uh, spoiler—Luke's father. That utterly complicates both his and Luke's mission and lends an emotional challenge that wasn't there before. Kylo Ren gets that complication earlier, right out of the gate with *The Force Awakens*—he's far more human than Vader is, and far earlier in his journey of transformation to the dark side, too. He's scary because he's familiar to us. He's scary because he's human—not some killing machine, but a person who believes—or who is gaslighting himself into believing—in the crusade he's undertaking. For me, a great villain is the sort that can have a conversation with the hero, because you know it's going to be *fascinating* conversation. When I look for examples of great

villains, one that I always come to is René Belloq from *Raiders of the Lost Ark*, every conversation he has with Indiana Jones reminds the audience that he's merely a shadowy reflection of our hero. Kylo Ren does the same for Han Solo, not only in their one scene together, but through every other interaction he has as well. We see that all of the elements that made Han Solo and Anakin Skywalker great characters separately combine to make a monster.

Kylo Ren is every bit the shadow of Luke as he is his own father and grandfather. Where Luke would rather kill himself than kill or join his father in the dark side, Kylo Ren would rather kill his father than embrace the light.

It's a stunning parallel that allows us to add Kylo Ren to the pantheon of *Star Wars* villains and we know that he will hold his own amongst that number."

MORE TO SAY

You can follow Bryan Young on twitter @swankmotron.

HAVE YOU?

CELEBRATION IV UPDATE
THE LATEST NEWS

THE INDY VAULT
EXPLORE THE ARCHIVES

CGI STAR WARS
SNEAK PEEK INSIDE!

STAR WARS

INSIDER

A LONG TIME AGO.....

STAR WARS: THE PAST, THE PRESENT, THE FUTURE!

PLUS: SEE THE LOST *STAR WARS* STORYBOARDS!
HOW *STAR WARS* BECAME PART OF THE LANGUAGE!
WEIRD COLLECTIBLES! YOUR *STAR WARS* MEMORIES!

THE ADVENTURE CONTINUES WITH *STAR WARS: THE FORCE UNLEASHED*

9 771754 075002

FORCE POWER!
UNLEASH YOUR INNER SITH

ISSUE 93
MAY/JUNE 2007

THIS MONTH, FAR, FAR AWAY....

Star Wars Celebration IV held in Los Angeles, California

Robot Chicken: Star Wars airs.

Legacy of the Force: Sacrifice released.

A groundbreaking experience that introduced the world to an intriguing new character, *Star Wars:* The Force Unleashed was an award-winning multi-platform video game that remains popular with fans to this day.. It tells the tale of Darth Vader as he plots against the Emperor by taking on a secret apprentice: Galen Marek, otherwise known as Starkiller, otherwise known as player one! The lightsaber action is fast and furious, but it's the astonishing realization of Force powers that really captured the imagination of fans and video gamers. Has there been a greater, more pleasing moment in a *Star Wars* game—or indeed any game—than using the Force to casually lift a hapless, panicking stormtrooper, fly him through the air, and then casually toss him to the ground?—**Jonathan Wilkins**

THE NEXT OFFICIAL INSTALLMENT IN THE *STAR WARS* SAGA!

UNLEASH YOUR INNER SITH!

DARE TO TAKE ON THE ROLE OF DARTH VADER'S SECRET APPRENTICE IN THE HIGHLY ANTICIPATED VIDEO GAME *STAR WARS: THE FORCE UNLEASHED* – AS THAT'S AS CLOSE AS YOU'LL GET TO BEING A REAL JEDI... OR SITH!

WORDS: FRANK PARIS

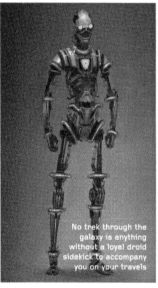

No trek through the galaxy is anything without a loyal droid sidekick to accompany you on your travels

I magine it's the summer of 1977. You're six years old and you're sitting next to your parents in a packed movie theater. In front of your wide eyes and blown up to awesome proportions, an old wizard says words to an idealistic farm boy that will set your imagination afire. "A young Jedi named Darth Vader... helped the Empire hunt down and destroy the Jedi Knights." Now imagine that somebody told you back then that almost 28 years later, when you're a full-grown adult, you'd sit in another packed theater seeing these very events unfold onscreen... Not only that, but what if that same person told you that a couple of years after that, not only would you *see* these events happen, but that you'd help *make* them happen? Most likely you'd look over your shoulder for the men in white suits...

However, that's exactly what LucasArts has store for *Star Wars* fans next year with its upcoming action/adventure video game, *Star Wars: The Force Unleashed (SW:TFU)*.

This is so much more than your average vi game, however! Scheduled to be released in early 2008 for 'next gen' and current gaming consoles, the game promises to be significant more than just the *Star Wars* franchise's initi foray into next-generation gaming.

This is nothing less than the next major *St Wars* entertainment event!

The Force Unleashed is the official next chapter in the core *Star Wars* saga, with mor story input from George Lucas than any previ game. With the game's release will be book a comic tie-ins, as well as a toy line from Hasbr

This concept piece shows Felucia a lush planet full of bizarre plantlife

BRIDGING THE SAGA

The storyline of the next *Star Wars* chapter will bridge the two film trilogies, taking place during what Obi-Wan Kenobi dubbed the 'dark times' between *Revenge of the Sith* and *A New Hope,* when the Empire is subjugating planetary systems with impunity and Darth Vader has settled into his role as a Sith Lord. You will play as a brand new character in the *Star Wars* mythos – a secret Sith apprentice of Vader's, clandestinely trained by the Dark Lord and unknown even to the Emperor. After honing your physical skills and warping your mind to the dark side of the Force, Vader has successfully forged you into a living instrument of terror and dispatches you to help exterminate the last Jedi stragglers who have remained hidden throughout the galaxy. Armed with a crimson-blade lightsaber and an uncanny mastery of the Force, you will use your skills for tracking, fighting and ultimately slaying the last remnants of the old Jedi order. And you will use a dizzying array of lightsaber skills and over-the-top Force powers.

The bull rancor is even more dangerous than the one seen in *Return of the Jedi...*

Haden Blackman, Project Lead of *Star Wars: The Force Unleashed*, spent months exploring different story ideas along with a team of developers, and frequent meetings with George Lucas, before LucasArts decided upon an epic that would explore the rich potential of the years between the two film trilogies, tie them both together, and introduce a major new character to the series. "It was one of several concepts that we brainstormed internally at LucasArts. We knew that we wanted to have a main character that uses the Force, focus on the era between Episodes III and IV, and include Vader in a significant way," says Blackman. "We developed several different concepts and focus tested each. The concept that seemed to resonate the strongest, and was the team's favorite, revolved around the secret apprentice."

Since *SW:TFU*'s storyline will be tightly meshed with that of the six movies, series creator George Lucas' heavy involvement with the game's direction was essential; he actively helped shape the storyline and its impact on the *Star Wars* universe – much more than on any other project in LucasArts' history. What has been most important to Lucas is that the game introduces new, compelling characters that will resonate with fans. "George provided a great deal of input on the types of

I encounter Shaak Ti, who is allied Force-wielding rancor riders.

SYNERGISTIC VISIONS

With both Industrial Light & Magic and LucasArts based at Letterman Digital Arts Center in San Francisco, the proximity of the two companies allows them to work jointly on certain projects. The first project to enjoy this synergy is *The Force Unleashed*. Not only will LucasArts use the same toolsets created by

ILM for films like *Pirates of the Caribbean III* in the game, but ILM technology will be used to create a number of visual effects. Among the ILM techniques will be facial animations and likeness captures, visual effects authoring, lighting, character performances, and graphics pipelines.

A prominent Jedi he Prequel Trilogy, haak Ti has exiled rself to the floral planet of Felucia.

Master Kota is among the Jedi who are being hunted by the Empire.

Maris Brood skillfully wields a new lightsaber variant.

STAR SCRIBE

If you're a follower of LucasArts games, or the voluminous Expanded Universe for that matter, the name Haden Blackman should be a familiar one. Not only has he worked on previous *Star Wars* games such as *Galaxies* and *Starfighter*, but he's also penned numerous books and comics, including a stellar *Clone Wars*-era run of the comic book series, *Republic*.

· He is Project Lead on *The Force Unleashed*, and is one of the game's main writers. "In comics, you basically have an unlimited budget based on the talent of the artists," he responds when asked how writing comics differs from writing games. "You can include a scene of a giant space station blowing apart, and not worry about how many animators, modelers, VFX artists, engineers, and others are required to pull it off – you're just relying on an artist, inker and colorist. In games, you can only build so many assets and sequences, and the more complex and action-oriented, the more difficult they are to achieve."

While pointing out the differences between the two media, Blackman does note a couple of similarities that demonstrate that no matter the medium, a good story is a good story. "A writer needs to be focused on economy of dialogue and to develop characters and convey critical information in as few words as possible."

characters we should include," says Blackman. "And (he) really pushed us to create new characters."

Although LucasArts is saving most surprises for closer to the game's release, we can reveal a few newcomers to the *Star Wars* saga. Joining your secret apprentice character will be Juno Eclipse, a female Imperial pilot and – as suggested by Lucas – a potential love interest. You will also be accompanied by a droid whose personality and functions will be revealed later. You will run across numerous surviving Jedi, a couple of whom are no doubt destined to become fan favorites. First is General Kota, a grizzled, militaristic Jedi General who survived the Jedi Purge – but not without scars. There's also Maris Brood, a powerful and deadly female Jedi.

Expect to see some familiar faces too. Fans will be happy to know that Togrutan Jedi Master Shaak Ti will triumphantly return to make a stand against your character on Felucia. Speaking of that Episode III planet, players will get their first-ever look at the fungus planet's indigenous inhabitants, plant-like creatures with masked faces and strong connections to the Living Force. Obviously Vader will factor heavily in the game, and when Vader is around, you can be sure that a certain cackling Sith Master isn't far behind.

"Taking the Force, a key element in *Star Wars*, and making it the protagonist of a strong *Star Wars* experience, will blow players away."

– Julio Torres, game producer

FULFILLING THE FORCE

The game's biggest star, however, is not a flesh and blood creature, but something more elusive yet paramount to *Star Wars'* cross-generational appeal: the Force. Explosively paced, over-the-top, no-holds barred Force battles are the crux of the gameplay and members of the development team are taking great pains to ensure that you will utilize the Force in ways never seen before. "Taking the Force, a key element in *Star Wars*, and making it the protagonist of a strong *Star Wars* experience, will blow players away," says Julio Torres, one of the game's producers.

Your character will start his adventure with four core Force powers – push, grip, repulse, and lightning – all of which will be amped up to staggering degrees. With these core abilities alone you'll be able to hurl Imperial stormtroopers through walls, pick up and toss large structures and even vehicles, and generate 360-degree shockwaves that destroy everything in their path. And that's not even mentioning other powers you will unlock throughout the game. Force powers can be combined with one another or with lightsaber attacks. For instance, you can levitate a stormtrooper off of the ground and hurl your lightsaber right through him. Or you can Force-push him into a pillar and when that pillar crumbles, grab large pieces of the rubble and hurl them at his squad mates. There will be few limits to the number of creative ways you can manipulate the environment, and other characters, with the Force.

To accomplish all of this, the development team will utilize the Havok physics engine and incorporate two major technologies never before seen in games. First is a program known as *euphoria*. Developed from a 'virtual stuntman' program, *euphoria* is a bio-mechanical artificial intelligence engine that imbues non-player characters with virtual nervous and muscular systems that react to stimuli. When attacked, these characters act out of self-preservation, behaving and reacting as actual people would – adapting differently on the fly in every way, each time.

The second innovation making its debut in *SW:TFU* is Digital Molecular Matter, or DMM for short. DMM can roughly be described as *euphoria* for in-game artificial matter. It grants environmental objects physical properties so that wood splinters, glass shatters, metal warps, plants bend and stone crumbles as they would in the real world, depending on the force and angle of an attack, and always in different ways. Like *euphoria*, this all occurs in real-time, not via animation.

Combined DMM and *euphoria* will not only greatly increase *SW:TFU's* replay value – you can play through levels over and over and never have the same experience twice – but will also raise the bar for character AI (artificial intelligence), environmental destructibility and interactivity in gaming. During a demo in which Vader's apprentice used the Force to hurl a huge piece of equipment against a gantry holding a group of Imperial troops, each of the hapless victims exhibited a completely unique reaction. Some braced for impact, others grabbed ledges to keep from falling, held nearby structures for support, or struggled to maintain balance as the area around them quaked. When the apprentice tossed objects directly at them, some raised their hands to protect themselves, while others deflected the attack or simply ducked out of the way.

Every *Star Wars* hero has his own iconic ship. In *The Force Unleashed*, the Secret Apprentice's is called the *Rogue Shadow*.

145

Left – No *Star Wars* game would be complete without stormtroopers.
Below Left – In-game character models such as this sandtrooper depict meticulous detail.

Familiar *Star Wars* vehicles such as the AT-ST may have gone through some modifications in *The Force Unleashed*.

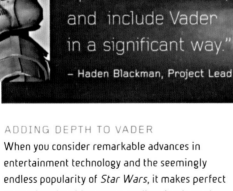

"We knew that we wanted to have a main character that uses the Force, focus on the era between Episodes III and IV, and include Vader in a significant way."

– Haden Blackman, Project Lead

Juno Eclipse is both an Imperial pilot and the Apprentice's love interest, but how that happens in the story remains a mystery.

ADDING DEPTH TO VADER

When you consider remarkable advances in entertainment technology and the seemingly endless popularity of *Star Wars*, it makes perfect sense that the video game medium is where the next major chapter of the *Star Wars* saga will be told. It is all the more fitting that LucasArts is going all out to deliver not only a major leap forward in gameplay and technical effects but, more importantly, a rich story that will offer new insights into, and have an impact on, a galaxy far, far away. After all, the main reason *Star Wars* has captivated generations of fans is its grand, sweeping story and enduring characters, and *The Force Unleashed* will be a great story in its own right, while also enhancing enjoyment of the films. "Hopefully, when you're done playing, you'll have a deeper understanding of both trilogies," says Blackman,

"and specifically new insight into Darth Vader as a character."

The Force Unleashed will follow the footsteps of the award-winning *Knights of the Old Republic* in that it will have multiple endings, with choices you make affecting characters' lives and ultimately the fate of the galaxy. If you're a stickler for continuity don't fret: Lucasfilm will decide to make one of the endings canon and that ending will be shared by the book and comic tie-ins. When asked what fans can look forward to the most, Torres says, "The depth of the main story, the character development, and of course the connections that are made with the first three Episodes and the last three Episodes. A great story like it has never been seen before, and coupled with the Force, it will make this next chapter of *Star Wars* worthy of any epic movie or story."

...You'll encounter Shaak Ti, who is allied with Force-wielding rancor riders.

Felucia has also been featured in *Star Wars: Episode III*, as well as *Star Wars Battlefront II*.

The Wookiee homeworld of Kashyyyk is just one of the exotic locales you'll visit in the game.

Natives of the planet Felucia, as first visualized in this concept art, wear masks composed of vegetation.

THE WORLDS OF *THE FORCE UNLEASHED*

No *Star Wars* adventure is worth its weight in Imperial credits without a robust amount of globe-hopping across the far reaches of the galaxy. In *The Force Unleashed* you will visit a large number of planets and installations during your search for the last of the Jedi. LucasArts will announce more locales at a later date, but for now, here are a few we know of:

Raxus Prime
This junk-ridden planet appeared in the *Clone Wars* video game as well as in comics and books. A grungy, polluted environment littered with junk and refuse, Raxus Prime offers huge possibilities in terms of the amount of objects that can be manipulated and wielded using the Force.

Felucia
Seen in *Revenge of the Sith*, the fungus planet is rife with the Living Force. This is where you, as Vader's secret apprentice, will encounter Shaak Ti, as well as a pack of vicious rancors.

TIE Fighter Construction Facility
While exploring this interstellar factory, players will get a look at how the Empire builds its massive fleet of TIE fighters.

Kashyyyk
A shadow has descended on the Wookiee home world as Imperial forces embark on a campaign to enslave the entire planet.

In *Star Wars: The Force Unleashed*, you are Darth Vader's Secret Apprentice.

You are Darth Vader's Secret Apprentice.

ASKING ANAKIN | EVIL DEEDS | THE OLD REPUBLIC

MATT LANTER INTERVIEWED ! | *STAR WARS'* DARKEST MOMENTS | WE PREVIEW THE GAME THAT WILL BLOW YOUR MIND!

VILLAINS
SPECIAL

STAR WARS

EXCLUSIVE
INTERVIEW!

**THE CLONE WARS
PRODUCER
CARY SILVER ON
SEASON TWO**

JOIN US!
THE VILLAINS OF STAR WARS

STAR WARS INSIDER
#113 Dec 2009
US $7.99 CAN $9.99

KILL KENOBI!
HOW THE FORCE UNLEASHED:
ULTIMATE SITH EDITION
IS REWRITING HISTORY!

SACKING OF CORUSCANT
THE OLD REPUBLIC

ISSUE 113
DECEMBER 2009

June 1, 2009. A hotly anticipated new *Star Wars* trailer that tells its own story is getting fans' blood pumping and their hearts racing. But this trailer, dubbed "Deceived," isn't for a movie release or an animated series. It's been created especially to promote a videogame: The Old Republic. It marks the debut of a terrifying new Sith Lord, Darth Malgus, voiced by Jamie Glover (whose father played General Veers in *The Empire Strikes Back*), and depicts events that take place 10 years prior to the in-game storyline. It was made using motion-capture technology, with fight choreography rendered in photo-realistic CGI. Far from being deceived, fans have learned that a new era of *Star Wars* gaming is about to begin!—**Jonathan Wilkins**

THIS MONTH, FAR, FAR AWAY....

The Clone Wars: Season Two began with the episodes "Holocron Heist" and "Cargo of Doom"

Star Wars: The Clone Wars: Republic Heroes released

Star Wars: The Clone Wars: Republic Heroes: Prima Official Game Guide released

Invasion: Refugees 4 released

The Clone Wars: "Children of the Force" aired

LEGO Star Wars: The Visual Dictionary released

Death Troopers released

Invasion 0: Refugees, Prologue released

The Clone Wars: "Senate Spy" aired

THE SACKING OF CORUSCANT

A behind the scenes look at the epic trailer for *Star Wars*: The Old Republic.

Words: David W. Collins.

There's little doubt that ardent *Star Wars* gaming fans are aware that LucasArts and Bioware—which previously collaborated on the 2006 hit Knights of the Old Republic—have again teamed to bring gamers *Star Wars*: The Old Republic, a massively multiplayer online video game (or MMO) set more than 3,000 years before the events of the six films.

Already gamers are chomping at the bit to sign up and discover what awaits them, with forums abuzz with great anticipation as fans look at video diaries, comics, concept art, and regular blog posts from members of the development team.

In June 2009, LucasArts and Bioware captured the attention of the entire gaming world and beyond by releasing a cinematic trailer that showed a glimpse of the game's story. More than just a three-minute peek into a new game, the trailer was a short film that told a chilling story about pivotal events that rock the *Star Wars* galaxy.

"Having story as the focus of this MMO is the entire reason for doing Star Wars: The Old Republic," says James Ohlen, Studio Creative Director and Lead Designer at Bioware, which is developing the game. "While story has appeared in many other MMOs, it has never been given the attention or love that you can find in a single-player game."

For the specially created trailer, Ohlen adds, "We wanted to have a movie that showcased one of the defining moments of the Old Republic era—the sacking of Coruscant by the Sith Empire.

"We also wanted to show the movie from the point of view of the Empire. *Star Wars*: The Old Republic is a *Star Wars* game that allows you to play on the side of evil, so we reflected that in the movie."

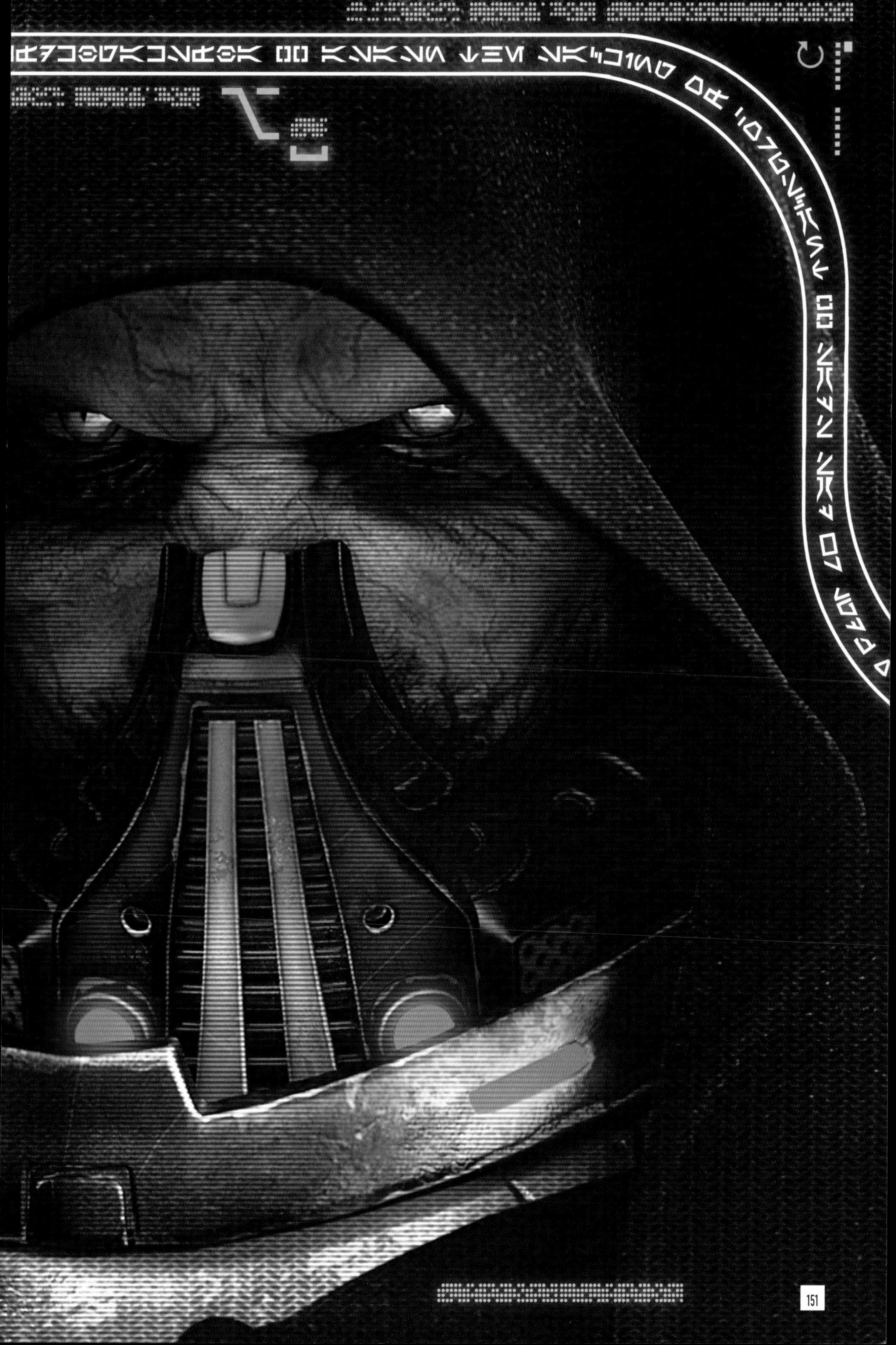

> "*Star Wars*: The Old Republic created a huge buzz at E3, with the trailer winning several 'Best-Of' awards."

MORE THAN A TRAILER

"We wanted more than just a trailer; we wanted to make a cinematic Star Wars experience," says Roger Evoy, Marketing Manager at LucasArts. "Star Wars: The Old Republic is a ground-breaking MMO, so we wanted a ground-breaking trailer." LucasArts and Bioware collaborated with Blur Studios of Venice, California to create a trailer that would create a buzz and represent the game's story. Multiple storyboards and scripts later, the stage was set for the sacking of Coruscant and a massive attack on the Jedi Temple by an army of Sith warriors.

In the trailer, we hear a Sith Lord's ominous voice say, "Our time has come. For 300 years, we prepared. We grew stronger." For the role, long-time talent directors Darragh O'Farrell and Will Beckman cast a British voice actor named Jamie Glover. "It's interesting to note that he is the son of Julian Glover, an actor that *Star Wars* fans know as General Veers from *The Empire Strikes Back*," says O'Farrell.

"The Sith warrior is designed for fans of Darth Vader," Ohlen adds from his office at Bioware. "When designing the class, we made a list of all the iconic moments from the movies that a Vader fan would want to experience. We used that list to inform how the Sith warrior story would play out and what abilities he would get."

Once the story and battle concepts were in place, Blur began the enormous task of using motion capture, key-frame animation, and sophisticated rendering to create photo-realistic visuals.

During this process, rough cuts and early versions called "animatics" were sent to LucasArts and Bioware for review.

"It was an incredibly collaborative process," remarks Evoy. "So many people offered amazing feedback during this project; Bioware and LucasArts folks primarily, but also from Lucas Licensing, and the director and producers at Blur; it was obvious that this trailer was shaping up to be something very special!"

"The Sith Warrior is designed for fans of Darth Vader."

⟨ᚱᚾ⟩ᚷᚢᚱᚾ⟩

SOUND STORY

a Sound Supervisor at LucasArts, this writer
to see a rough cut of the "Deceived" trailer
early 2009. I immediately asked if I could
the Sound Lead on the project, and went
out setting up the sound team. We knew
t we wanted to work in close collaboration
h Skywalker Sound, due to the cinematic
ture of the trailer. We treated it just like
lm: We walked Foley (created sound
ects) at Skywalker Ranch for the sounds
haracter movements like footsteps, body-
s, costume swishes, and props. Next, we
ed a group of actors and held an ADR (or
oping") session at Skywalker Sound's
hestral scoring stage, a space that could
ture the echoes heard inside the great hall
he Jedi Temple. This allowed us to create the
formances needed for a giant battle, as all of
actors brought the Jedi and Sith armies to life!
We brought in long-time collaborator Erik
reman (a *Star Wars* veteran in his own right,
ving won an Emmy for his work on the *Star Wars:
ne Wars* micro-series from 2003), and the team

began the sound design and editorial process. Once
all of the pieces came together (along with the near-
complete visuals), we began work on the audio mix.
The "Deceived" trailer was set to debut the first
week of June, and we couldn't wait to see how
gamers and *Star Wars* fans would react.
And what a reaction it was! The trailer
captured the imagination of gamers and *Star
Wars* fans alike, and *Star Wars: The Old Republic*
created a huge buzz at E3, with the trailer
winning several "Best-Of" awards, and setting
fans' excitement at fever pitch.
"When we decided to go with Blur we were
pretty sure we were going to get quality work,
but that didn't prepare us for the end result,"
says Bioware's Ohlen. "We were blown away
by what they delivered."
"You want to know what the best part about this
is? This trailer is just the tip of the iceberg," adds
LucasArts' Evoy. "Just wait until the game comes
out: gamers and *Star Wars* fans are going to
lose their minds." ◆

⟨ EXPANDED UNIVERSE - FOR MORE INFORMATION, GO TO **WWW.SWTOR.COM**

EXCLUSIVE LIMITED EDITION COLLECTOR'S COVER
STAR WARS®
INSIDER
STAR WARS INSIDER#113
Dec 2009
US $7.99 CAN $9.99

DARTH KRAYT
A LEGENDARY SITH

ISSUE 113
DECEMBER 2009

THIS MONTH, FAR, FAR AWAY....

Imperial Commando: 501st released

Star Wars: The Complete Vader released in Canada and the United Kingdom

Legacy 41: Rogue's End released

Star Wars: The Clone Wars: The Official Episode Guide: Season 1 released

Though he is now something of a myth in *Star Wars* lore, Darth Krayt was once a key figure in the *Star Wars* Expanded Universe after making his debut in Dark Horse Comics' *Star Wars: Republic* series in 1999. Krayt was developed by author Timothy Truman, who skillfully concealed the character's true identity across five years of comic-book storytelling. This led to much speculation among fans, with the final reveal in *Star Wars: Legacy* in 2007 doing nothing to diminish Darth Krayt's legend.—**Jonathan Wilkins**

> "The galaxy writhes in chaos and disorder. It requires a man vision. I am that man."
>
> —Darth Krayt's words upon seizing the Imperial throne

Often overlooked by history is the fact that the true power of the Galactic Empire was a Sith Lord. Remarkably, after the defeat of Palpatine/Darth Sidious it took more than a century before a new dictator—Darth Krayt—put the galaxy back under the yoke of the dark side of the Force.

Born A'Sharad Hett on Tatooine, Krayt was a Jedi hero long before he felt the call of the Sith. His human mother and father lived among the Tusken Raiders and A'Sharad became part of their culture, too. Like the other Tuskens, he learned to ride a bantha, kept his body concealed behind tight wraps

and a sand-filtering breath mask, and fought a ferocious krayt dragon during his trial of adulthood. Because his father Sharad Hett had once been a great Jedi, A'Sharad possessed the same ability to touch the Force.

The bounty hunter Aurra Sing killed Sharad Hett while A'Sharad was still a teenager. Orphaned, A'Sharad found a new family among the Jedi Order. As the apprentice of Ki-Adi Mundi, A'Sharad wielded his father's lightsaber in defense of the Republic. He eventually found an opportunity to take his revenge on Aurra Sing, but refused to strike a killing blow after defeating her in combat.

Profile by Daniel Wallace

KRAYT

IMPERIAL KNIGHTS! SAVE YOUR EMPEROR!

AGGH!

THE CLONE WARS

Though his restraint showed maturity, he still struggled with the violent urges of his upbringing. The Jedi Council believed that he could learn more from the Dark Woman—the Jedi who had once trained Aurra Sing—and his apprenticeship was transferred to her. In time, he took on his own Padawan, a Nikto named Bhat Jul.

The Clone Wars gave A'Sharad an opportunity to deploy his combat prowess. He distinguished himself as a battlefield commander and a leader of clone soldiers, though the death of Bhat Jul saddened him. On a mission to Aargonar, A'Sharad teamed with Anakin Skywalker, who hated all Tusken Raiders due to the torture and death of his mother Shmi. In a tense reconciliation, A'Sharad learned the secret of Anakin's Tusken massacre, and Anakin became one of the few to see A'Sharad's real face beneath his mask.

During the Outer Rim Sieges, A'Sharad fought at Boz Pity and Saleucami. He survived the betrayal of his clone troops during Order 66 and escaped to Tatooine, where he took up his former life as a Tusken chieftain. Obi-Wan Kenobi, now living on Tatooine as a hermit, confronted A'Sharad over Tusken aggression toward the local moisture farmers. A'Sharad lost an arm in the encounter, which shamed him in front of his clan. A bitter A'Sharad ventured out into the galaxy as a bounty hunter, journeying to the sinister world of Korriban.

There he encountered the long-dead spirit of the Sith Lord XoXaan. Bereft of the guidance of his father, his Jedi mentors, or his Tusken comrades, the secrets of the dark side held particular appeal for A'Sharad. Shortly after this encounter, A'Sharad became a prisoner of the extragalactic aggressors known as the Yuuzhan Vong, who tortured him inside the agonizing restraints of the Embrace of Pain. Vergere, a fellow ex-Jedi who now lived among the Vong, seemed to reinforce the teachings of XoXaan by pointing out the folly of shutting out the totality of the Force by only focusing on its light side. By the time he left the Vong, A'Sharad vowed to reestablish the Sith Order with himself as ruler.

To mark the start of his plan he adopted the Sith name Darth Krayt after the proud predators of his birth world. He had no patience for the "Rule of Two" espoused by Emperor Palpatine, and promised to attract many Sith Lords under a single banner with his new One Sith philosophy, the "One Sith" being the Sith Order itself. Once organized, their sheer number would prove more than a match for the reinvigorated Jedi Order that had sprouted under Luke Skywalker's leadership. Building such a cabal would require secrecy and time, but fortunately he had both. Biological enhancements received during his Yuuzhan Vong captivity extended Krayt's life far beyond its normal span.

DESCRIPTION

All his life, Darth Krayt kept himself hidden behind a mask. His true face bore the black lines of traditional Tusken tattooing, but he wore a Tusken Raider sand helmet even during his training sessions inside Coruscant's Jedi Temple. After his transformation into Darth Krayt, he wore a heavy covering of Yuuzhan Vong living armor that bore wicked protrusions and bony spikes and left nothing visible save his mouth and eyes. Krayt perfected his combat techniques over many decades, and his skills with telekinesis and Sith lightning far outstripped those of any Sith of his era.

SEIZING THE THRONE

More than 100 years after the fall of the Empire, Darth Krayt engineered a pact with the new Empire. He arranged for the sabotage of a joint Jedi/Yuuzhan Vong terraforming project, triggering a new Galactic Civil War. The One Sith finally emerged from the shadows as Imperial allies, but Krayt wasn't about to stop there. After the Imperial capture of Coruscant, Krayt seized the throne from Emperor Roan Fel and ordered the massacre of the Jedi. For a decade Krayt ruled known space, using agents such as Darth Talon and Darth Maladi to crush resistance and to keep Roan Fel's surviving "Empire in exile" in check.

In the year 137 after the Battle of Yavin, Darth Krayt could no longer ignore the deterioration of his ancient body. He became obsessed with Cade Skywalker—the Jedi descendent of Anakin and Luke who had turned his back on his heritage—under the belief that Skywalker's Force-healing abilities could save him from death. He captured Skywalker on Coruscant and tried to recruit him to the One Sith, but the young Force-user escaped.

Krayt found his kingdom disintegrating along with his body. Brutal strikes by Roan Fel's forces and the meddlesome Galactic Alliance Remnant led to a humiliating defeat at the Mon Calamari shipyards. As payback, Krayt ordered the near extermination of the Mon Cal species.

On Had Abbadon, in the Deep Core, Krayt confronted Skywalker a second time. But a third Force-user possessed powers that outshone them both. Karness Muur, an ancient Sith spirit, blasted Krayt with overpowering energy, sending him over a cliff to the rocks below.

Still alive, Krayt looked to his aide Darth Wyyrlok for help, but Wyyrlok executed his helpless Master in a Sith power grab. a

VOTE **STAR WARS!** **DETAILS INSIDE!**

BEST VILLAIN?

BEST HERO?

STAR WARS

AMAZING NEW
FICTION

RALPH
McQUARRIE
REMEMBERED

ISSUE 134
JULY 2012
U.S. $7.99
Can $9.99

TITAN

STAR WARS
CLONE WARS

SEASON 5 EXCLUSIVE!

10 GREAT MOMENTS FROM SEASON 4

Episode titles revealed! New details teased!

SPEAK LIKE A SITH
LEARN THE LANGUAGE OF EVIL

ISSUE 134
JULY 2012

It says something about the intricate detail that goes into *Star Wars* that the Sith have their own decipherable language. Linguistics expert Ben Grossblatt was called upon to create a language from scratch for the *Book of the Sith*, which was published in 2011. *Insider's* wonderfully in-depth look at the language might not make you fluent in dark side dialogues, but it might just help you master some key Sith sayings. Nwul!*—**Jonathan Wilkins**

*Peace!

Speak like a Sith

SITH LANGUAGE CREATOR BEN GROSSBLATT OFFERS A CRASH COURSE ON THE FINER POINTS OF THE MOST EVIL LANGUAGE IN THE GALAXY!

In November, 2010, I was given an assignment right up my alley: Invent a Sith language for *Book of Sith*, a collection of Sith history, philosophy, and artifacts (available from Amazon).

My goal in developing Sith was to create a plausible, linguistically sound language. Plausible, in that it would sound and feel real—not like a cartoonish language for the bad guys to speak. (I wouldn't be putting sentences like *Glotch blug bodge!* in the mouths of the Sith.) Linguistically sound, in that it would conform to patterns and principles of (human) language. This is the way to achieve a language with the depth and richness that the *Star Wars* galaxy demands.

I faced more practical considerations, too. For instance, Sith had to look pronounceable. Otherwise, no one would even bother trying to speak it. The words would just lie there on the page. I knew that Sith would have no "words" like *r'rhhoqtk*.

The first step was settling on what linguists call a segment inventory—a list of the phonemes (speech sounds) employed by a language. Combined with a system of phonotactics (the ways phonemes are put together), this would give the Sith language its personality, its unique feel. In order for the language to come alive and embody fans' ideas of the Sith, the language would need to be realistic, of course, but it would also need to *sound right*.

Sith needed to feel martial and mystical. You had to be able to imagine it carved into temple façades, painted on tattered banners, and yelled from parapets. It needed to work as a suitable, aesthetically-pleasing vehicle for communication among the feared and misunderstood Sith—for curses, chants, conspiracies. To that end, I imagined a tough—but not barbarous—language, one that could convey a kind of confident elegant cruelty. And Sith would have to ring with authority so you could envision it functioning among elites of the dark side the way Latin functioned in Europe for centuries: as a repository of culture and learning.

To achieve a formal, quasi-military quality, I preferred the frequent use of closed syllables (syllables ending with consonants) to make brisk, choppy word

chwûq	"ember"
hâsk	"anguish"
ajak	"doctrine"

A note for language nerds

In rendering Sith words in the Roman alphabet, I use two special symbols: [û] stands for the vowel sound in *club*. [â] stands for the vowel sound in *bash*. Those symbols aren't part of the IPA (International Phonetic Alphabet), but I wanted to avoid symbols that "civilians" would find completely unfamiliar.

Giving Sith a mystical feel was more of an art than a science. I hoped to evoke a kind of ancient strangeness with consonant clusters like nw-, dzw-, and tsy-.

nwûl	"peace"
dzwol	"to exist, abide"
tsyoq	"to squeeze with the hand"

Translation headaches

Because of its limited phonetic palette, creating Sith versions of *Star Wars* names can be tricky. Take the name *Palpatine*. Sith doesn't have a "p" sound, and no Sith words have an "ee" sound in a closed syllable or an *l* between consonants. The closest a Sith speaker with a heavy accent could come to replicating the Emperor's name might be *Marmûtin* (or "mar-muh-tin"). I like to think creative Sith scribes would translate His Excellency's name into their own language. If the basis of his name was the same as the word *palpitare* ("to throb"), then the Sith equivalent of his name might be *Chirikyât* ("chee-ree-kyatt"), or "He Who Causes Them to Throb and Tremble in Fear."

The Knotters of Entrails (alchemists who created Sithspawn, as described in *Book of Sith*) would be known in Sith as *Ninûshwodzakut*. That jawbreaker is built from four separate chunks, like so:

nin	+ûsh	+ wodza	+ kut
"tie, knot"	agentive marker	"intestines"	collective plural marker

The phrase "because of dreaming about a demon" is rendered in Sith as a single, towering word—*kûskutsiqsayanjat*:

kûsk	+ ut	+ siqsa	+ anjat
"to dream"	nominal marker (of verbs)	"demon"	ablative marker

Given that Sith might have appeared on pedestals and pillars, and in the dark declarations of tyrants, I wanted the words themselves to be like monuments. Imposing, undeniable. Words like steles recording the names of sinister heroes. To my mind, long, intricate words suggested something about the language's structure; Sith would be an agglutinative language. That is, a language, like Turkish, that builds words by

Accent these lexical Goliaths on the first syllable—every Sith word is stressed that way—and they take on a looming, teetering quality, as if they might collapse

Sith Scribing

Beyond these and other abstract concepts that appealed to the linguistics wonk in me, there was also a writing system to invent. I wanted this version of Sith writing to lend itself to calligraphy—the *Book of Sith* Holocron contained a scrap of Sith burial shroud, after all—as well as to printing and inscribing (imagine 10-foot-high Sith letters chiseled into stone slabs).

The Sith alphabet (the Kittât):

t	d	k	q	m	n	ts	dz	s	z	h	ch	j	sh	r/l	w	y

i	"heat" "hit"
â	"hat"
u	"suit" "soot"
û	"hut"
o	"toad"
a	"ah"
oi	"toy"
ai	"buy"

Note that some consonants combine with w and y to form complex characters:

tw, dw, mw, nw, tsw, dzw, ty, dy, my, ny, tsy, dzy

Putting it all together—the phonology, the morphology, the syntax, and the writing system—means we can produce things like this, the Sith version of the Rule of Two:

The Rule of Two
Chwayatyun

chwayat	+ yun
"rule, law"	+ "two"

Two there should be;
Dzworokka yun

dzwol	+ okka	yun
"to exist, abide"	+ hortatory mood	"two "

no more, no less.
nyâshqûwai, nwiqûwai

nyâsh	+ qû	+ wai	nwi	+ qû	+ wai
"big, much, many"	+ comparative	+ negation	"small, few"	+ comparative	+ negation

One to embody power,
Wotok tsawakmidwanottoi.

wo	+ tok	tsawak	+ midwan	+ ottoi
"one"	+ ordinal number marker	"embodiment"	"power"	dative marker

the other to crave it.
Yuntok hyarutmidwanottoi.

yun	+ tok	hyal	+ ut	+ midwan	+ ottoi
"two"	ordinal number marker	"to crave"	nominal marker (of verbs)	"power"	dative marker

There's more to say about Sith (and *in* Sith), but these basics are enough to express the mood and character of the language of the dark side.

Qorit ("The End")

Ben Grossblatt is a senior editor at becker&mayer!, the bookmakers who developed and produced Book of Sith *and its Holocron case as well as* Jedi Path. *Ben discovered* Star Wars *in 1977 and earned a Master's degree in linguistics in '97. His last name translated into Sith is* Dzunyâsh.

DON'T TRUST THE JEDI?
WHY THE FORCE ISN'T *ALWAYS* WITH YOU!

COMING SOON
WHAT *NOT* TO MISS IN 2012!

STAR WARS
INSIDER

VOICE OF THE CLONES
DEE BRADLEY BAKER
ON BEING AN
ARMY
OF ONE!

TALES FROM THE
DARK SIDE!
**THE STORY
OF DARTH
PLAGUEIS
REVEALED**

POWERFUL
FRIENDS!

MEET THE CHARACTERS OF
STAR WARS: THE OLD REPUBLIC

ISSUE 130
JANUARY 2012
US $7.99 CAN $9.99

TITAN

FAMILY TRADITION
REJECTING THE JEDI TEACHINGS

You need only take a cursory look at Jason Fry's *Star Wars* output to see that he is extremely well-versed in its lore. Such is his expertise that he was able to pull together a fascinating feature charting how and why Anakin fell to the dark side, while Luke avoided such a fall from grace. Fry is very good at challenging set ideas you might have about the saga, and with this thoughtful piece he will have you re-watching the movies with fresh eyes.—**Jonathan Wilkins**

THIS MONTH, FAR, FAR AWAY....

Star Wars: The Wrath of Darth Maul released

LEGO Star Wars: The Padawan Menace released

LEGO Star Wars: Anakin: Space Pilot released

Star Wars: The Phantom Menace 3D Storybook released

LEGO Star Wars: Darth Maul's Mission released.

Darth Vader stunt performer Bob Anderson dies at the age of 89

The Clone Wars: "Escape from Kadavo" aired

Darth Plagueis released

The *Star Wars: Legacy—War* trade paperback released.

Knights of the Old Republic: War 1 released

FAMILY TRADITION

Was Anakin's change to the dark side provoked by the Jedi's aversion to emotion? Jason Fry abandons his Jedi teachings and digs deep.

"You must unlearn what you have learned."

That's Yoda's advice for Luke Skywalker, novice Jedi in training. But it's also good advice about Yoda's own teachings. One of the underappreciated themes of the *Star Wars* saga is how the Jedi's own traditions lead to their ruin, and how Luke saves the galaxy by refusing to follow those traditions, rejecting his Masters' teachings, and trusting his feelings.

That theme was present in the three movies of the original trilogy. But the prequels have deepened our awareness of it, showing us how Anakin Skywalker and the Jedi Order were at odds from the very beginning and helping explain why he fell—and how his son redeemed him.

Consider our first view of the Jedi Council in Episode I *The Phantom Menace*. Anakin, separated from his mother Shmi and still in shock, is tested by a circle of intimidating Jedi Masters. When Yoda asks how he feels, Anakin replies, "Cold, sir." It's an apt description of how he's treated. When Anakin admits he misses his mother, a scornful Yoda says he's scared to lose her.

Angry, Anakin asks what that has to do with anything, and Yoda warns that fear leads to anger, anger leads to hate, and hate leads to suffering.

It's a line *Star Wars* fans love to quote, but consider the context: Yoda accuses a frightened child of being vulnerable to the dark side because he misses his mother.

Rejected by the Jedi and facing an uncertain future—Will he be marooned on Coruscant? Returned to Tatooine?—Anakin meekly tells Qui-Gon Jinn that he doesn't want to be a burden. But he must have remembered that first encounter with the Jedi during his Padawan years.

At the end of *The Phantom Menace*, Obi-Wan Kenobi defiantly tells Yoda he will honor Qui-Gon Jinn's dying wish and train Anakin—whether or not the Council agrees. Obi-Wan gets his wish, but the greatest obstacle he faces isn't Anakin's preternatural ability with the Force, or Obi-Wan's lack of experience as a teacher. Rather, it's that Anakin knew his mother and Obi-Wan never did. Anakin must struggle with an emotional bond that Obi-Wan cannot understand.

Anakin meets the Jedi.

Qui-Gon is known for defying the Council, and is kind to Anakin. But even he seems more concerned with Anakin's Jedi potential than with oppression on Tatooine. Qui-Gon doesn't regard freeing slaves as his business, and doesn't think twice about removing Anakin from his mother, who is left in slavery. The wealthy, powerful Jedi Order could easily have sent Jedi back to Tatooine to free Shmi, but we know from *Attack of the Clones* that this never happens.

If Qui-Gon had lived, perhaps he would have arranged for Shmi to be freed, and been more sympathetic to Anakin's unique background. But he dies, and Anakin proves a difficult pupil for Obi-Wan and a rebellious Padawan. It's easy to imagine him fuming about his mother, abandoned as the property of Watto the Toydarian, while the Jedi Council sends him to help Obi-Wan with border disputes.

Anakin's downfall begins in Episode II *Attack of the Clones*. The movie chronicles his growing love for Padmé Amidala, memorably captured by a teaser poster that declares "A Jedi shall not know anger. Nor hatred. Nor love." In Episode II, Anakin's love for Padmé leads him

astray, but it's the threat to Shmi that leads him into darkness. Anakin's mother is now the wife of Cliegg Lars, a moisture farmer who bought her from Watto and freed her. She has been captured by vicious Tusken Raiders, and her torment reverberates in the Force, reaching Anakin through his dreams.

Don't look back! Anakin faces his destiny.

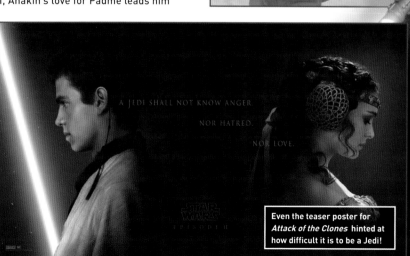

A JEDI SHALL NOT KNOW ANGER.

NOR HATRED.

NOR LOVE.

Even the teaser poster for *Attack of the Clones* hinted at how difficult it is to be a Jedi!

Anger and the inability to let go collide when Anakin witnesses the death of Shmi in *Attack of the Clones.*

Anakin finds Shmi, but she dies in his arms, and he slaughters the Tusken Raiders who imprisoned her. Through the Force, Yoda and Mace Windu sense Anakin's pain—and Yoda hears the voice of Qui-Gon imploring Anakin to stop—but they can do nothing. It is Padmé who tries to comfort Anakin, reminding him that he's only human. Anakin's reply is chilling: "No, I'm a Jedi."

Standing at his mother's grave, Anakin laments that he wasn't strong enough to save Shmi, and vows not to fail his loved ones again. That vow has terrible consequences, as we see in Episode III *Revenge of the Sith.* Anakin is haunted by a vision of Padmé—whom he has secretly married—dying in childbirth. This may strike us as the kind of nightmare that's normal for a young man awaiting the birth of a child, but we have to remember Anakin's abilities with the Force: As Qui-Gon notes in Episode I, Anakin can see things before they happen. For Anakin, premonitions are predictions, and painfully accurate ones.

In Episode III, Anakin is driven to desperate measures to save Padmé, and ultimately loses her because of his own actions. But he turns to the dark side only when he thinks he has no other choice. First, Anakin confides in Yoda about his premonitions, without saying whom he's concerned about. Yoda's reply is useless for a terrified husband and father-to-be: "Death is a natural part of life. Rejoice for those around you who transform into the Force. Mourn them, do not. Miss them, do not.... Train yourself to let go of everything you fear to lose."

Anakin hears this cold advice in misery—and the Jedi Council then betrays him, as he sees it, by refusing to grant him the rank of Jedi Master. A frustrated Anakin is easy prey for the whisperings of Darth Sidious, disguised as Chancellor Palpatine. Palpatine says the Sith Lord Darth Plagueis could keep those he loved from dying, and Anakin's desperate hunger for this knowledge and power in the Force is what leads him to betray Mace Windu, become Darth Vader, and massacre the Jedi. His attack on Padmé leads to her death as Luke and Leia are born—the very thing Anakin sought to prevent.

The original trilogy is about Luke discovering his true parentage and

Palpatine at his most manipulative in *Revenge of the Sith.*

Mace Windu: The final barrier between Anakin and the dark side!

Luke's Jedi training on Dagobah holds many challenges, but should Yoda's teaching be observed?

learning the ways of the Force. But it isn't the Jedi code that helps Luke end the Sith's rule. Rather, he succeeds because he rejects the teachings of Yoda and Obi-Wan, representing the old Jedi Order. The Jedi failed to see the danger awaiting Anakin because they rejected or couldn't understand love and family. Luke succeeds because he embraces love and family, reawakening the good in his father, who then destroys Darth Sidious to save his son.

In Episode IV *A New Hope*, Luke learns the ways of the Force from Obi-Wan, who leaves exile on Tatooine in an effort to save Princess Leia Organa, Luke's secret twin sister. But Obi-Wan lies to him about his father's identity. Yoda later claims Luke wasn't ready for the burden of that terrible knowledge, but it also seems likely that Obi-Wan wanted to avoid the emotional attachment between child and parent, remembering that helped doom Anakin.

In Episode V *The Empire Strikes Back*, Luke becomes Yoda's Padawan, and there

are echoes of Anakin's training and the dilemmas he faced. Like Anakin, Luke is told he is too old to begin the training. Like Anakin, he has a vision of his loved ones suffering in captivity, and receives cold advice from Yoda, who tells him to sacrifice Han and Leia if he honors what they fight for. Like Anakin, Luke's attempt to rescue his friends backfires: He is nearly killed by Vader, and his friends must risk their lives to rescue him (after they had already succeeded in saving themselves, except for Han).

In Episode VI *Return of the Jedi*, things come full circle. But it's easy to miss that Luke disagrees sharply with his Jedi teachers about what to do. Obi-Wan and Yoda have trained Luke and push him toward a second confrontation with Vader. He is, they believe, the Jedi weapon that will destroy both Vader and the Emperor. When Luke insists there is still good in Vader, Obi-Wan retorts that "he's more machine than man—twisted

"I know there is good in you." Luke defies the Jedi and redeems his father.

IN THE EXPANDED UNIVERSE

Many stories in the Expanded Universe beyond the movies deal with love, the Jedi code, and the Skywalkers' struggle with their passions.

The Jedi's reasons for rejecting Anakin for training are further explained in the back-story of Episode I. The Jedi take children from their parents very early, to prevent them from forming emotional attachments that they fear could cloud their judgment and prevent them from serving as impartial arbiters in galactic disputes.

In *The Clone Wars* series, Obi-Wan discusses the unrequited love between him and Mandalore's Duchess Satine, telling Anakin that when Yoda says a Jedi must not form attachments, "he usually leaves out the undercurrent of remorse." And Jude Watson's *Jedi Apprentice* books introduce strong attachments between Qui-Gon Jinn and the Jedi Master Tahl, and between Obi-Wan Kenobi and his fellow Padawan Siri Tachi.

Siri Tachi

Karen Traviss created a rogue Jedi named Djinn Altis who rejects the Jedi teachings, allowing Jedi to form romantic attachments. Several of Traviss' novels contrast the Jedi attitude toward attachments with the tight family and clan bonds of Mandalorian culture.

Matthew Stover's Episode III novelization fills in a crucial part of the reason for Anakin's fall, and explains his fury at not being named a Jedi Master, a plot point that struck some movie viewers as office politics. As Stover explains, the Jedi's most-secret lore is restricted to Masters, and Anakin believes this lore includes how to save Padmé. When the Council refuses to make him a Master, his hopes of using this information disappear, and Darth Sidious has the opening he needs to convert him to the dark side.

The family bonds that are so important in *Return of the Jedi* are further explored in *Dark Empire*, the 1991 Dark Horse comic

eries written by Tom Veitch. Luke's
eed to understand why Anakin fell
eads him to confront Sidious, reborn
hrough Force sorcery—and like Anakin,
e is ensnared. In *Dark Empire*, Luke is
aved by his sister's love, rather than by
is father's: Leia joins her Jedi powers
vith Luke's, and Sidious' destructive
orce storm washes over the Skywalker
wins, rebounding on its creator and
estroying him.

It's a deepening of *Return of the Jedi*'s
esson. That moment binds Luke and
eia together as Skywalkers and saves
hem, as the climax of *Return of the Jedi*
ound Luke and Anakin and saved them.
)nce again, the keys to the Skywalkers'
ictory are love
nd family.

Rejecting the dark side, Luke faces
the wrath of the Emperor.

and evil." When Luke says he can't kill
his own father, Obi-Wan despairs, "Then
the Emperor has already won."

But Obi-Wan could not be more
wrong. It is precisely because
Luke can't kill his own father
that he defeats the Sith. On Endor,
Luke reaches the man behind the
mask by addressing Vader as
father and as Anakin Skywalker.
Vader rejects that name, saying it
"No longer has any meaning for
me," but he sounds regretful when
he tells Luke that "It is too late
for me, son."

It isn't. Aboard
the second Death Star,
Luke pulls back from
the dark side, refusing to
kill Anakin and take
his place as Sidious'
apprentice. He tells
the Emperor that "I am
a Jedi, like my father
before me." Rejected,
Sidious tries to destroy

Luke—but he forgets
about the fallen
Anakin. Anakin has
already endured
Sidious manipulating
him into losing his
wife; now, he sacrifices
himself to save his
son, hurling his Master
into the Death Star
reactor shaft. He at
last brings balance
to the Force, as prophesied long ago. It
isn't Jedi teachings that save the galaxy,
but bonds the Jedi tried to forbid—such
as the love of a father for his son and a
son for his father.

Emotional attachments, in other words. ☮

*Jason Fry is the author and co-author of
more than a dozen* Star Wars *books,
including* The Essential Atlas *and* The
Essential Guide to Warfare. *He lives in
Brooklyn, N.Y., with his wife, son and about
a metric ton of* Star Wars *stuff.*

A Jedi redeemed!

The climactic struggle between
Luke and Vader.

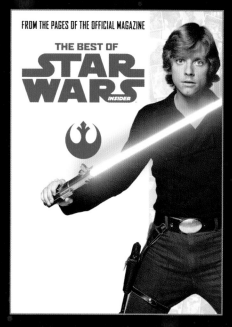
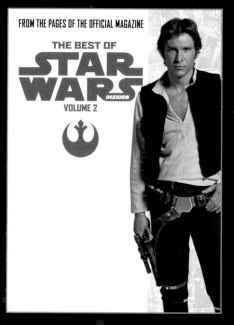
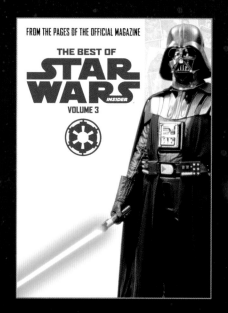
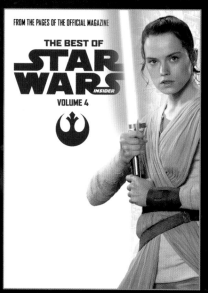